ENRIQUE'S JOURNEY

Sonia Nazario

AUTHORED by Melanie R. McBride
UPDATED AND REVISED by S.R. Cedars

COVER DESIGN by Table XI Partners LLC
COVER PHOTO by Olivia Verma and © 2005 GradeSaver, LLC

BOOK DESIGN by Table XI Partners LLC

Published by GradeSaver LLC, www.gradesaver.com

First published in the United States of America by GradeSaver LLC. 2012

ISBN 978-1-60259-323-7

Printed in the United States of America

Table of Contents

Table of Contents

Biography of Nazario, Sonia (1960-N/A)

Though she is best known for her book *Enrique's Journey*, Sonia Nazario has had a distinguished career as an award-winning journalist and writer.

Nazario was born on September 8, 1960, in Madison, Wisconsin, to Argentinean immigrants. Her father, Mahafud, was born in Argentina and is of Syrian descent. Her mother Clara was born in Poland, but fled to Argentina during WWII to escape persecution. Nazario's parents emigrated to the United States in 1960. Her father wanted to escape Argentina's militaristic government, which suppressed academic freedom. Nazario was raised in both Kansas and in Buenos Aires.

Nazario earned her B.A. in History from Williams College in 1982, and her M.A. in Latin American Studies from the University of California, Berkeley in 1988. In 2010, she was awarded an honorary doctorate from Mt. St. Mary's College. Nazario initially worked as a staff reporter for the *Wall Street Journal*, covering social issues from New York, Miami, Atlanta, and Los Angeles for over ten years. She began working for the *Los Angeles Times* in 1993 as a reporter for projects and urban affairs.

Nazario has won numerous awards for her journalism, including the George Polk Award for Local Reporting in 1994, for "The Hunger Wars -- Fighting for Food in Southern California." "Orphans of Addiction" was a 1998 Pulitzer Prize finalist, and winner of the National Council on Crime and Delinquency PASS Award. Nazario also won the National Council on Alcoholism and Drug Dependence of the San Fernando Valley Special Recognition Award for her article "Sobering Facts" in 1999. She won the Pulitzer Prize for feature writing for her series "Enrique's Journey," first published in *The Los Angeles Times* in 2002. In 2012, Nazario was listed among the "40 Women Who Changed Media Business in the Past Forty Years" by *Columbia Journalism Review*.

About Enrique's Journey

Enrique's Journey first appeared in 2002 in the *Los Angeles Times*, as a series of six articles written by Sonia Nazario, with accompanying photographs by Don Bartletti. Both author and photographer were awarded the Pulitzer Prize for their work. Nazario later expanded the article into a book, which was published by Random House in 2006. Since then, *Enrique's Journey* has won numerous book awards, and is on the required reading list of a number of colleges and high schools across the country.

Nazario was inspired to write *Enrique's Journey* after discovering that her friend and maid, Carmen, had left her four children behind in Guatemala so that she could earn money in the U.S. to support them. When Carmen's son Minor later arrived, having braved a journey fraught with dangers, he told Nazario about *El Tren de la Muerte* (The Train of Death) that migrants must brave to make it to the U.S.

Nazario soon discovered that Carmen and Minor's story was not uncommon among the immigrants who arrive in the United States illegally from Central America and Mexico each year. In fact, she realized, it was particularly common for single mothers and their children. To illustrate this changing face of immigration, Nazario began a five year investigation into the lives of migrants traveling to the United States from Central America. In order to give a human face to her work, she chose to retrace the steps of one child's journey north. By centering her book around a central narrative, she maintains the journalistic freedom to explore the myriad questions of immigration without losing dramatic momentum.

Enrique's Journey is, at its core, the story of one young man's odyssey. Over eight attempts north, Enrique travels from Honduras to the United States, guided by only his wits and his hope to reunite with his mother. Like many children who take the same journey, Enrique faces numerous challenges including starvation, dehydration, the dangers of the trains, the harsh weather conditions, the brutality of the gangsters, and the negligence of the immigration authorities and police. Despite the odds, Enrique refuses to give up and finally reaches the United States to reunite with his mother.

Nazario's book is by no means a political tract, and the author mostly avoids expressing any strong opinions. Instead, her intention is clearly to ask the right questions, and influence the immigration debate in the U.S. so that it includes not only economic and social factors, but also the human, individual ones.

Character List

Belky

Lourdes's first child, and Enrique's sister. Belky grew up in the care of her Aunt Rosa Amalia and Uncle Carlos. She eventually has a child of her own, and helps raise Enrique's daughter Jasmín.

El Brujo

A member of the MS gang who befriends Enrique on the freight trains. It is this friendship that spares Enrique from being targeted by gang members.

Carlos

Enrique's uncle, and husband to Rosa Amalia. He tries to help Enrique sort through his troubles in Honduras, and sets him up with a job at a tire store.

Carmen

Sonia Nazario's maid, whose story inspired the author to write *Enrique's Journey*.

Diana

Lourdes's daughter with her ex boyfriend, Santos. Diana was born in the United States.

Enrique

The protagonist of the story. Plagued by his mother's abandonment, Enrique leaves Honduras and braves the difficult journey north to reunite with Lourdes. Though Enrique has many personal problems - a drug addiction and serious resentments among them - he is also defined by his persistence, bravery, and incredible sense of hope.

Hipolito Reyes Larios

The bishop in Veracruz who inspires his parishioners to help the Central American migrants by showing them mercy and charity.

Jasmín

Enrique and María Isabel's young daughter. Her existence becomes the motivation for Enrique's final journey, to become a father worthy of respect.

Jóse

Enrique's friend who accompanies him on his first failed attempt to the United States.

Lourdes

Mother of Belky, Enrique, and Diana. Lourdes left her children in Honduras to seek better employment opportunities in the United States. She lived in poverty most of her life, working menial jobs to send money home to her family. Lourdes always had faith that Enrique would one day return to her, but has trouble overcoming his resentments once he arrives.

Marìa Marcos

Enrique's paternal grandmother, who helped raise him as a child. Though generous, she has trouble battling his rebellious attitude and has to send him elsewhere.

Marìa Isabel

Enrique's girlfriend, Jasmín's mother. Marìa Isabel eventually joins Enrique in the United States, leaving her young daughter in Honduras.

Mirian

Lourdes's sister, who also travels to the United State seeking better employment with the hope of returning to Honduras and her children.

Minor

Carmen's son, whose story of traveling through Mexico inspires Sonia Nazario to write *Enrique's Journey*.

Olga

Director of the Shelter of Jesus the Good Shepherd in Tapachula, Mexico. She helps migrants who have been severely injured by the trains. She is guided by her faith in God, and works tirelessly to ease the physical and spiritual struggles of the migrants.

Padre Leo

A disheveled but lovable priest who is called "the champion" by migrants. He arranges meals, phone calls, clothing donations, and housing for migrants in Nuevo Laredo.

Rosa Amalia

Lourdes' sister who raises Belky in her absence. Rosa Amalia is married to Carlos.

El Tiríndaro

A smuggler in Nuevo Laredo who takes Enrique across the border. He is a heroin addict who bribes local police officers so he can make money smuggling. He was killed in 2002.

Santos

A boyfriend of Lourdes, who lives with her in the U.S. and fathers Diana. He eventually disappears, presumably killed on a subsequent attempt to sneak into the U.S.

Marco

Lourdes's brother, with whom Enrique lives for a while in Honduras. Marco is a strong presence in the boy's life until he dies.

Major Themes

Family

Without a doubt, family is the central theme of *Enrique's Journey*. By basing her investigation around Enrique's story, Nazario explores the ways that immigration affects individual families.

Lourdes believes she is acting responsibly by traveling to the U.S. for work. Though she makes the trip for the sake of her children, they immediately feel the pangs of separation. Their whole notion of "family" becomes jaded. Who is their parent, or as Enrique asks, "Dónde está mi mami? Where is my mom?" Because of her decision, both mother and child suffer loss.

In the wake of separation, all concerned are led to create new family structures, often unhealthy ones. Enrique's father starts another family, leaving Enrique doubly deserted and starting a spiral that leaves him to be traded from home to home. He wants to get his girlfriend pregnant largely because it might satiate his feelings of abandonment.

Meanwhile, Lourdes creates a new life for herself in the U.S. with her daughter Diana, but finds her life is incomplete without Enrique and Belky. Overall, the family unit itself is endangered, and this is one of Nazario's overall points. Even when they are reunited, their various resentments made a true reunion difficult. When Enrique makes his own journey and asks Maria Isabel to join him, he risks starting the same cycle of abandonment with his own daughter, suggesting that these decisions are not easily criticized, but rather must be considered as one of many factors at risk in the immigration debate.

Abandonment

At various points of the book, Enrique is abandoned by every significant parental figure in his life. First, Lourdes emigrates to the United States, leaving a five year old Enrique to be raised by his irresponsible father. Then, his father leaves to begin a new family, after which he is traded from home to home, largely because of the rebellious attitude that forms in response to the abandonment. In many ways, it is adolescent confusion over this abandonment that inspires Enrique to brave the significant risks of the journey to reunite with a mother he barely knows. Though this pain does inspire Enrique to fear repeating the cycle, he does abandon María Isabel, his girlfriend, who is pregnant with their child. The theme of abandonment comes full circle when Enrique and María Isabel leave their daughter in Honduras while they create a new life together in the United States. Enrique's greatest hope is that he can bring his daughter to him and not prove guilty of the same offenses that corrupted him in his youth.

Journey

As the title of the book suggests, a main theme within the narration is that of the journey. Enrique must travel thousands of miles in order to reach his destination, his mother. His journey is one of suffering and fear, of pain and longing. Through the lens of the author's narration, we follow in Enrique's footsteps as he overcomes each obstacle. The physical aspect of his journey challenges his body, as seen during his recovery from the injuries he sustained at the hands of the six men on the train.

However, Enrique's journey is not only physical, but also mental as he grows from a boy to a man. His anger, resentment, and feelings of abandonment fuel his confrontations with his mother. There are times in the book when he falls victim to his own shortcomings: doing drugs, tantalizing his mother, mismanaging his finances. His emotional journey concludes when, after he is reunited for a second time with his mother in Florida, Enrique reveals that he will stop living in the past, and will save enough money to bring María Isabel into the country so that they might work together to bring happiness into their daughter's life. He is ready to take yet another journey, this time marked by responsibility instead of adolescent rebellion and resentment.

Love

Although it is not overtly stated in the text, love is one of the greatest motivations that drives the characters. Enrique travels thousands of miles to reach his mother because he believes she is the only one who still cares for him. Lourdes makes the incredibly difficult decision to leave her home, her children, and the only life she has ever known, all in the name of love. Through their actions, characters reveal how terribly they feel the absence of love. Enrique falls in love with María Isabel, who "loses herself in Enrique." The two conceive a child together, and although Enrique is not physically in Jasmín's life, the promise of bettering her life leads him to take control of himself.

Poverty

Characters in this book must make many difficult decisions in order to deal with their debilitating poverty. Lourdes remembers too well the pain of her childhood poverty, and so refuses to let her children suffer it. As a result, she ironically must abandon them to take care of them - she sees no other option. Similarly, Enrique is willing to suffer the poverty of the journey in order to find greater wealth up north, wealth with which he can prove himself responsible and take care of his girlfriend and child.

However, one of the book's interesting counterpoints is the reminder that the U.S. contains its own threat of poverty. Lourdes works a series of menial jobs that disappear frequently, and has to weather many disgusting circumstances to survive. As the final chapter and afterword illustrate, the desire to escape poverty force families to make very difficult decisions that are ultimately not in their best interest.

Immigration

Though the book is centered around Enrique's journey, its larger purpose is to examine the various approaches to immigration, in hopes of creating social awareness. Nazario's intention, clearly stated in her prologue, is manifest in the way she juxtaposes the protagonist's tale with interviews and details of other migrants and the many institutions they encounter on their journeys. By the end of the book, Nazario is directly confronting the questions of immigration. In the afteword, she examines how immigration affects the economy, the family unit, the community, and institutions like public schools. She is not interested in answering questions, but rather in asking them. This approach makes sense considering the complicated factors she explores through Enrique's journey - so much is at stake for both these individuals and their communities that a simple answer would surely ring false.

Hope

Behind the entire book sits the theme of hope - without it, most of the amazing accomplishment would not be possible. Enrique admits he lacks any faith that God will help him on his journey, as he has been too sinful. Instead, he relies on his own determination and skill to see him through. He finds hope in himself, in the distant idea of his mother, and in the other migrants who encourage one other. He sees defeat everywhere, but refuses to be discouraged.

Especially during the sections of the book devoted to the journey, Nazario explores the many places from which migrants get home. They are inspired by kindness from citizens, especially in places like Veracruz, where strangers run alongside the trains and toss up much needed food and clothing. They also find it in charity, given by the many churches and shelters devoted to their welfare. Nazario takes extra time to discuss particularly kind individuals like Padre Leo or Olga, largely because they help the reader understand how migrants can maintain their hope. However, most profound of all is the hope that migrants like Enrique have to reunite with their loved ones. The promise of Lourdes is the largest motivation he has.

Glossary of Terms

bandit
a robber

combi
mini bus

detention center
a facility which houses detained illegal immigrants

el Bus de Lágrimas
translation for "the Bus of Tears"

el Manguito
a dangerous immigration checkpoint

el Norte
translation for "the North," which indicates Mexico and then the U.S. for Central Americans

fichera
prostitute

gangster
a member of a group of criminals who commit brutal crimes against migrants

Grupo Beta
a group associated with the Instituto Nacional de Migración that rescues Central American migrants in Mexico

hitchhiker
someone who solicits rides from strangers

Immigration and Naturalization Services (INS)
a bureau of the U.S. Department of Justice that regulates the admission of foreign-born persons entering the United States of America

impetus
an impulse or incentive

jefe
translation for "boss, manager"

la bestia
translation for "the beast," referring to the Mexican state of Chiapas

la migra
a colloquial name for the officers of the Mexican Border Patrol

lempiras
Honduran currency

Mara Salvatrucha
one of the many gangs that intimidates migrants on top of the trains headed north

mi hijo
translation for "my son"

migrant
a person who travels to find work or to relocate

pesos
units of Mexican currency

smuggler
someone who is paid to help migrants cross the border

U.S. Border Patrol
a law enforcement agency with the INS that prevents illegal entrance into the United States

Short Summary

Enrique's Journey chronicles the life of a young Central American boy, and his quest to reunite with a mother who left him at the age of five to find work in the United States.

Enrique's mother, Lourdes, struggles in Honduras to support her young children, Belky and Enrique. She knows she will not be able to send her son and daughter to school past the third grade, and does not want them to grow up as she did, in extreme poverty. Like many other single Latina mothers in the recent decades, Lourdes leaves her home and family to travel to the United States so that she might send money home for her children.

Young Enrique has no idea why his mother has left, and his family in Honduras does not give him straight answers. Over the years, Enrique is shuffled from one family home to another, while his sister Belky attends a good school and is well cared for by their aunt. Enrique is forced to sell food and spices when still a child, in order to help pay for family expenses. He lives with his paternal grandmother for most of his young life, but is eventually kicked out of her home when he begins to rebel. Frustrated with his mother, his own issues of abandonment, and the death of his beloved uncle, Enrique turns to drugs for comfort. His family and his girlfriend, María Isabel, try to intervene but make little headway.

In the meantime, Lourdes discovers that life in the United States is more difficult than she expected. She works a series of low-paying jobs, and becomes pregnant. After she gives birth to her daughter, Diana, Lourdes loses her factory job, and becomes a fichera, a type of prostitute. Eventually, she finds steady work again, and is able to send money, clothing, and toys to her children in Honduras.

Although Enrique and Belky appreciate the gifts, they are no substitute for their mother's physical presence. Enrique's drug problems continue to escalate until his drug dealer threatens to kill his cousin over unpaid debts. Enrique steals his aunt's jewelry to pay off his dealer, but is caught by the police. Later, he is kicked out of his home again, and although he does not want to leave María Isabel, who is pregnant with their child, Enrique feels compelled to journey to his mother, the only person he believes might understand and love him.

So begins Enrique's journey through Central America and Mexico on his way to the United States. He departs with little money, a change of clothes, and his mother's phone number written on a scrap of paper. Enrique attempts the dangerous journey eight times before he succeeds. During his first seven attempts, he is severely beaten, robbed, deported, and humiliated. However, he never gives up.

To travel north, Enrique, like other migrants, rides the tops of freight trains, a most dangerous endeavor. Many migrants have been killed on the trains, by being pulled under the wheels or by falling off. Gangsters rule the tops of the trains, robbing, beating, raping, and killing migrants. Bandits and robbers are also a threat. Equally dangerous are corrupt police officers and *la migra*, the Mexican immigration officers who have been known to rob migrants before deporting them. Lastly, migrants must weather the threats of starvation, dehydration, and exhaustion. Many migrants fail to make it as far as the U.S./Mexican border, but Enrique is not one of them.

On his eighth attempt north, Enrique waits on the banks of the Rio Grande in Nuevo Laredo, Mexico. It is a dangerous setting, but he is protected as part of a small encampment. He raises enough money to call his mother, who helps pay for a smuggler to take him across the river and into the United States. Enrique crosses the river in an inner tube and is taken to Orlando, Florida. He is soon reunited with his mother for the first time in over a decade. He and Lourdes embrace each other, but they do not cry. Soon enough, he moves in with Lourdes and her roommates, and begins to work.

The idealized reunion they both imagined is soon shattered by reality. Like many children who travel north to find their parent(s) in the United States, Enrique had created a larger than life image of his mother; he felt that if he found her, all of his troubles would go away. Lourdes, on the other hand, expects respect for the sacrifices she had made, but is met only with resentment and occasional cruelty. Enrique returns to using drugs and alcohol as a means of coping with his disappointment.

Meanwhile María Isabel is raising their daughter, Jasmín, in Honduras. Enrique, like Lourdes before him, sends money to his girlfriend and baby. Enrique wants to save enough money to hire a smuggler to bring María Isabel to the Untied States, so that they might work together to provide a better life for their daughter. Initially his personal problems and conflict with Lourdes distract him from sending much money back. However, time passes and he comes to peace with his resentments, and saves more. After these few years of indecision and miscommunication, Enrique pays a smuggler to bring María Isabel to the United States. Jasmín remains in Honduras, to be cared for by Belky.

Throughout *Enrique's Journey*, Sonia Nazario exposes the harsh realities of immigration. In many ways, her own perspective is as much a character as Enrique is. She suggests that the separation between a mother and her child, as experienced by Lourdes and Enrique, is not beneficial in the long run. Resentment, anger, and frustration lead to lasting emotional damage and misunderstandings. Nazario also explores the many questions - political, social, economic, and personal - of immigration through interviews and explanations as Enrique makes his journey. However, these many problems are ultimately presented as less profound than that of family deterioration.

Quotes and Analysis

"'Dónde está mi mami?' Enrique cries, over and over. 'Where is my mom?'"

Enrique to his family, 5

These haunting words, spoken by Enrique when his mother first leaves, touch at the center of the book's themes. No one tells five year old Enrique where his mother has gone, or when she is coming back. Lourdes and Enrique's long distance relationship consists of telephone calls and short letters. This particular quote resonates throughout the text as Enrique travels from Honduras to the United States in search of his mother, having no idea what she looks like anymore, where she lives, or if he will ever reach her. Implicitly, these words reveal the depth of abandonment, since this sentiment of longing will serve as motivation for Enrique to pass through a terrible ordeal.

"The single mothers who are coming to this country, and the children who follow them, are changing the face of immigration to the United States."

The author, xxv

In this quote, the author explains her purpose and inspiration for writing the book. Sonia Nazario wrote *Enrique's Journey* to shed new light on the broader issue of immigration in the United States. In order to bring a human face to her investigation, she chose to follow one boy's journey. This approach lets her make an implicit statement to any Latina mothers who are considering immigrating to the United States - in the end, the separation of parent and child might not be worth it. The resentment the children feel toward their mothers never really goes away. Similarly, the guilt the mothers feel for having left their children also persists. Even after mother and child are reunited in the U.S., new issues arise, often resulting in negative consequences. Nazario does not want to write a political book - she wants to put a new "face" on the issue by exploring its personal, individual side.

"This is what they get for doing this journey."

Adan DÃ–az Ruiz to Carlos Carrasco, 47

This quote is spoken in the time period directly after Enrique was savagely beaten and robbed by six men on the train, and reveals one obstacle migrants must face: the resentments of Mexican citizens. The mayor and townspeople of Las Anonas, in Oaxaca, Mexico have gathered to stare at him after his beating. Some are kind and give him money, while others look on in disgust. The mayor of a neighboring town utters this statement, specifically referring to the many injured and dead migrants he has dealt with over the years. Díaz decides to take Enrique to a local hospital not from kindness, but from pragmatism - it is cheaper for the community to treat him than it would be to bury him. Díaz's distaste is disturbing but not uncommon in this part of Mexico. Some Mexicans believe Central Americans have no business being in Mexico at all. They are concerned with their own economic problems, and have little sympathy for the problems brought by others. Their racism blinds them to the plight of the Central American migrant.

"In spite of everything, Enrique has failed again - he will not reach the United States this time, either. He tells himself over and over that he'll just have to try again."

The author, 60

Enrique's determination to reunite with his mother is an underlying theme of the novel. Here, he is being deported to Guatemala for the last time. He sits on the Bus of Tears, with other migrants who have been caught, and wonders whether the threat is worthwhile. He has already sacrificed so much. Ultimately, though, the many arguments for giving up matter less than his determination to reunite with his mother. If he lacked even a bit of such perseverance, he would surely be deterred as many others are. This sense of determination in the face of such extreme odds is one of the many sides of immigration that Nazario wants to present and explore.

"They really screwed me up."

Enrique to himself, 100

Enrique looks into a store window, and sees for the first time his battered reflection. He has been beaten, robbed, and humiliated. The scars on his head and body bear testament to what he has endured on this journey. When he looks into the window, he is ashamed by what he sees, and acknowledges that he is now marked by violence. However, he does not give up, but rather accepts this as another obstacle that he must overcome in order to succeed. His hope and determination are stronger than the troubles, and in confronting his own weakness but persisting nevertheless, he reveals that quality that ultimately facilitates his arrival in the U.S.

"It's wrong for our government to send people back to Central America. If we don't want to be stopped from going into the United States, how can we stop Central Americans in our country?"

A man from Veracruz to Sonia Nazario, 103

This quotation addresses the larger issue of immigration within the text. As the author states, a number of Americans believe that Central American and Mexican immigrants are taking jobs away from native-born citizens, are over-using government aid, and are bringing crime into the country. Some Mexicans, in turn, feel similarly about the Central Americans in their country. And yet this man's opinion touches on an unsettling hypocrisy that suggests a wider truth. It is within our human nature to want to protect what is ours. Most societies are reluctant to share their resources, and yet we usually recognize a duty to help our fellow man. Whereas an individual might acknowledge a flaw in his society's policy, the society as a whole cannot be so easily led to practice such idealism.

"Can you imagine how far they have come?"

The people of Veracruz to the author, 106

Unlike the citizens of many other states in Mexico, the people of Veracruz are known for their unwavering kindness toward migrants. Their priests and bishops encourage them to feed and clothe the migrants. They are reminded that Jesus himself was once a migrant, moving from Israel to Egypt. The migrants, in turn, view Veracruz as a land of hope and faith. Having passed through "the beast" of Chiapas, migrants are welcomed by the hope and kindness of Veracruz. Because this one part of Mexico is willing to show regular charity, many migrants are given the strength to continue that that might otherwise lose. This statement suggests that empathy can exist if we are willing to consider the migrants as individuals and not just faceless parts of a social problem.

"Thank you for returning to your country."

American Border Patrol officers to migrants, 137

These words have been heard hundreds of thousands of times by the migrants on the Mexican side of the Rio Grande. Enrique hears them as well. Certainly, they are representative of the final great obstacle migrants face - crossing the border into the U.S. However, the horizon in their sight is a symbol of hope, and this implicit warning functions in the same way. Although the Border Patrol agents offer constant reminder of their presence, there is also a tantalizing hope that if a migrant can avoid the Border Patrol, he or she can cross into the promised land and end this journey. They can change their country from Mexico to the U.S. with just a little bit of luck.

"The effect of immigration has been family disintegration. People are leaving behind the most important value: family unity."

Oscar Escalada HernÃ¡ndez to author, 248

This sentiment touches on what is arguably the book's primary purpose. Referring to the lasting emotional damage of family separation, Oscar Escalada Hernández, director of the Casa YMCA shelter for immigrant children, suggests that dissolution of the family is the worst effect of immigration. The separation between mother and child creates irreparable emotional damage that impacts not only those involved but also the community in which they interact. Nazario explains how some children grow into restless adults, who are never able to forgive their parent(s) for leaving them. Others, like Enrique, try to overlook the past and move toward a brighter future; however, their lives are often marked by addiction or other coping methods. The true irony is the fact that the mothers originally left their country and children to help keep their family intact. Little did they realize the future ramification of that decision. One of Nazario's purposes is to remind us all of this less palpable risk that migrant parents run.

"We'll have to leave the baby behind."

Enrique to MarÃ–a Isabel, 196

In a sad turn of events, María Isabel decides to leave her daughter, Jasmín, in Honduras while she joins Enrique in the United States. Enrique and María Isabel feel they are giving their daughter the best possible opportunity for the future. Yet, as Nazario insinuates in the Epilogue, this decision suggests that a vicious circle is continuing. Enrique's journey morphed from a trip through Mexico into a trip through himself, an attempt to make peace with his resentment over abandonment. And yet he and María Isabel repeat the same destructive pattern by leaving their daughter, with only hope of reuniting. Belky stands as a counterpoint, someone who actually does return to Honduras to raise her son, while Enrique persists in his hope that his family unit will not be too damaged by separation.

Summary and Analysis of Prologue

Summary

The author, Sonia Nazario, was at her home in Los Angeles on a Friday morning. When her maid, María del Carmen Ferrez, arrived, they began to talk of children. Sonia was shocked to learn that Carmen had four children who still lived in Guatemala.

Carmen's story began like those of many other single Latina mothers from Mexico and Central America who have traveled to the United States in search of a better life for their families. After Carmen's husband left her for another woman, she decided to travel to the U.S. in search of work. Leaving her children behind in Guatemala, Carmen embarked on a dangerous journey north, eventually arriving in Los Angeles. She now sends clothing and money back to her children, but feels the emotional strain of separation.

The following year, Carmen's son Minor arrived unannounced in Los Angeles. He had traveled from Guatemala to California, having faced threats, robbery and the shame of begging in order to reunite with Carmen and determine whether she still loved him. Nazario was intrigued by their story, and so began to investigate why so many Latina mothers and children are immigrating to the U.S. The author states that there is an insatiable need in the United States for cheap service and domestic workers. Every year, approximately 700,000 immigrants arrive in the U.S. illegally, while nearly a million others enter legally or eventually become citizens. The recent wave of immigrants from Central America and Mexico is historically unique - as the divorce rate in Latin America has risen, so have more mothers become unable to support their children and hence decided to brave the journey.

The same increase in immigration occurred during the 1960s and 1970s, when so many American women began working outside of the home for the first time. Responding to a need for cheap labor, floods of women from the Caribbean and Central America arrived in the U.S. to work as nannies and in nursing homes. In the 1980s, the number of domestic workers within Los Angeles doubled. Nazario states, "a University of Southern California study showed, 82 percent of live-in nannies and one in four housecleaners are mothers who still have at least one child in their home country" (xiv).

The U.S. has a complex history concerning immigration. The author states that the presence of immigrants in the U.S. "is deemed good or bad, depending on the perspective" (xiv). Nazario theorized that if she were to tell the story of one immigrant's journey, perhaps it would better illustrate the issue of immigration as a whole.

Nazario began to research the harrowing journey that young children from Central America and Mexico take. Usually, they travel on the tops of trains which they call *El Tren de la Muente* (The Train of Death), in the hopes of reaching their mothers in the United States. First, Nazario learned everything she could about the journey and its dangers, such as the "gangsters who rule the train tops," "the bandits along the tracks," the Mexican police who "rob and rape," and most importantly, the risk of "loosing a leg while getting on and off a moving train" (xv).

Nazario understood the threats of the journey. She was told of a man who lost his foot in the wheels of the train, and of a young girl thrown to her death by the gangsters. She knew she could get herself killed. In preparation for her trip, she laid down rules for herself, such as promising never to jump from a moving train (a rule she only broke once). She obtained a letter from the personal assistant of the President of Mexico, which promised her the cooperation of Mexican police/authorities during her investigation. The letter kept her out of jail three times. She also instructed the train conductors to watch for her while she was onboard. They would know her by her red jacket.

Nazario talked to dozens of children being held by the U.S. Immigration and Naturalization Services (INS) in California and Texas. She decided, after speaking to the children who rode on the trains, that instead of following one child's journey, she would reconstruct the trail of a child who had already successfully made it to the United States.

Nazario next needed to locate a child who had made the journey. She went to shelters and churches that took in immigrant children, and eventually found Enrique in Nuevo Laredo, on the banks of the Rio Grande in Mexico. She learned everything she could of Enrique's life, including details on his family and on his motivation for finding his mother. Traveling to Honduras and to Enrique's home, Nazario interviewed his family and retraced his route all the way to the United States.

Traveling over 1,600 miles in Enrique's footsteps, Nazario encountered gangsters, and regularly feared being robbed, beaten, and raped. She almost fell off the top of a train when a branch struck her in the face, and she in fact later learned that a child had fallen off the same train and had presumably died. Nazario watched as a train derailed in front of her, she witnessed a kidnapping, and she took part in a high speed chase. Nazario was often hungry, wet, dirty, cold, and miserable. However, she always knew that what she was experiencing was only a portion of what the children on the trains went through - she could always quit.

Because of her own heritage as a child of Argentinean immigrants, Nazario understands the desire for the freedom of the United States. She believes that "no number of border guards will deter children like Enrique" from entering the U.S. (xxiv).

Nazario ends her *Prologue* by stating, "Children who set out on this journey usually don't make it. They end up back in Central America, defeated. Enrique was determined to be with his mother again. Would he make it?" (xxvi).

Analysis

The Prologue introduces the style of the author's narration, a cross between traditional storytelling and investigative journalism. The examination of one young immigrant's journey, coupled with Nazario's own experiences as she retraces Enrique's steps, provides first-hand knowledge of the perilous journey north that so many Mexican and Central American men, women, and children take each year in the hopes of entering the United States. By exploring the intricacies of the journey itself, Enrique's story gives a face and a name to the often abstract, misunderstood topic of immigration.

The book's structure is chronological - in fact, it begins with Nazario's first exposure to the trend of mothers leaving their children behind. It will later follow her own journey in reconstructing Enrique's struggle. Once Enrique becomes a protagonist, it follows his own chronology. However, the structure also employs a type of journalistic omniscience; interspersed throughout the text are relevant statistics, other immigration stories, and corroborating evidence to support Enrique's personal insights. Similarly, the tone and setting change as Enrique's circumstances do; for instance, the setting of Mexico City and its tone is vastly different than that of Honduras.

The Prologue also serves to illustrate the many dangers of the journey. As Nazario lists the cautionary preparations she undertook to ensure her own safety, she establishes a dramatic quality for the reader. By introducing us to the many threats, we expect at any time that the characters we meet might perish under them. Part of what makes the book successful is that it can balance itself between journalistic investigation and dramatic story.

Nazario's own presence in the story also personalizes it. For instance, while traveling, Nazario gathered testimonials from migrants about their experiences. Nazario describes her interview with a fifteen year old girl named Karen, who had been raped in the same place that Nazario herself had visited the day before. Because of this interview, Nazario had recurring nightmares in which she was being pursued on a train, was in danger of being raped. By including her personal insight and reflections, Nazario creates an open dialogue with the reader, inviting discussion and analysis.

Nazario's work was originally published in the *Los Angeles Times* in 2002, as a series of articles which went on to win the Pulitzer Prize for Feature Writing. To expand the work, Nazario conducted hundreds of interviews in the United States, Honduras, Guatemala, and Mexico. She interviewed Enrique's family, friends, and anyone willing to collaborate. She traced Enrique's route twice, and traveled through thirteen states in Mexico. Her experiences on the train, at checkpoints, and at migrant shelters all enhance the narrative, by lending credence to the certainty of her tone. For instance, her description of the Nuevo Laredo encampment paints a clearer picture of what Enrique endured to get to the United States than a purely second-hand account would have painted. This allows the reader not only to learn of Enrique's journey, but to walk with him somewhat. It makes Enrique into both a real human being and a character in a narrative.

Summary and Analysis of The Boy Left Behind

Summary

Lourdes has decided to leave Tegucigalpa, Honduras for the United States. She is frightened for her son, five-year old Enrique, but she does not hug him or say a word as he clutches her pant leg. She cannot take his picture with her because it will break her resolve, and Lourdes knows she must leave if she is to earn a decent wage with which to create a better life for herself and her children.

In Tegucigalpa, Lourdes can barely afford food and clothing for her two children, Enrique and his seven-year old sister, Belky. Lourdes is a single mother at twenty-four years old. She washes other people's clothes in the river for money, and sells tortillas, used clothing, and plantains. Next to the Pizza Hut in downtown Tegucigalpa, she squats at the side of the road to sells gum, crackers, and cigarettes. Her future is bleak, and she knows she cannot afford to send her children to school past the third grade.

When she was seven years old, Lourdes saw images of New York City, Las Vegas, and Disneyland on the televisions at other people's houses. The dream of living in America, so far from a two room shack made of wooden slates with no bathroom, is thrilling for her.

Like many other women of similar circumstances, she decides to embark on the dangerous journey north, to find work in the United States so that she might send the money to her children. She plans to leave for one year, and then to return home. She has asked her sister, Rosa Amalia, to care for Belky while she is gone, and expects Enrique's father to take care of him. Lourdes does not say goodbye to Enrique - it is too hard for her. Instead, she tells him something he will always remember: "Don't forget to go to church this afternoon" (5). It is January 29, 1989, and Lourdes never returns.

The separation between mother and son dictates Enrique's future. He will eventually set out after her, and become one of 48,000 children from Mexico or Central America who enter the U.S. illegally. Nazario details this phenomenon. Most children who travel north are looking for their mothers, while others seek work or are escaping abusive homes. Half of them travel with smugglers, and the rest go alone. Hunted like animals by gangs, bandits, and corrupt police, the children are often robbed, beaten, and raped several times. Some are killed. Setting out with little money and often only a tentative idea of where their mothers live, the children cling to the tops of freight trains. To avoid the Mexican and U.S. authorities, they jump from moving trains, and sometimes fall into the wheels.

Though fifteen is the average age for migrants, children as young as seven travel alone, using only their wits and determination to guide them. Their mothers often leave when they are young, and these migrants begin to idealize them, believing their mothers to be larger than life. "Finding them becomes the quest for the Holy Grail" (7).

Lourdes travels with a smuggler, and crosses into the United States during of the largest immigrant waves in U.S. history. She enters the country at night through a sewage tunnel, and makes her way into Los Angeles. Her plan is to go to Miami, but her smuggler abandons her at a Greyhound bus station. She waits three days for him to return, but hunger and desperation drive her to find a job at a factory. There, she sorts tomatoes for $14.00 a day. Eventually, she locates a friend of her brother in Los Angeles who helps her obtain a counterfeit Social Security card and a job. Working as a live-in nanny, she moves into a Beverly Hills home to care for a three year old who reminds of her Enrique. Her employers pay her $125 a week, and Lourdes is able to send money, clothes, and toys to her children in Honduras.

Back in Honduras, Enrique asks after his mother everyday, but she does not return. His father remarries and moves out to start a new family. Enrique is left in the care of his paternal grandmother, María Marcos, and eventually grows to hate his father. Belky is living with Rosa Amalia in a nicer part of town, and is able to attend school thanks to the money Lourdes sends. Although she loves the clothing and stuffed animals her mother has given to her, she is deeply distraught by her mother's absence and finds comfort in befriending other young girls whose mothers have left.

The home Enrique shares with María Marcos is considerably less refined than that of Rosa Amalia. It is a four room hut built from wooden slates, with minimal electricity. There is no running water; the bathroom is a hole in the ground next to two large buckets used for bathing. Lourdes sends $50-$100 a month, but it is not enough for school supplies. Both Enrique and his grandmother work - she sells used clothing, and he sells tamales, spices, and plastic bags filled with juice.

Enrique makes a Mother's Day card for his grandmother, and rarely speak to Lourdes anymore. They do not have a phone, and he can only speak to her when she calls their cousin's home, but he is often not close enough to fetch when she calls. One year, Lourdes does not call at all.

Lourdes is struggling with her life in the U.S., and finds that the television images she once saw do not reflect reality. She now shares an apartment with three other women, and sleeps on the floor. An old boyfriend from Honduras, Santos, moves in with her and she unintentionally gets pregnant. Now working in a fish factory, Lourdes struggles through the pregnancy and a difficult relationship with her boyfriend. Santos does not take her to the hospital when she goes into labor; instead, he spends the night at a bar. She gives birth their daughter, Diana, and is only allowed to stay at the hospital for two days.

Two months after Diana's birth, Lourdes is fired from her job at the factory. She gets a new job at a pizzeria and bar. One night, Santos punches her in the chest because he is jealous of her friendship with one of her male coworkers. A year later, Santos returns to Honduras with their savings of several thousand dollars to make investments. He squanders the money on a drinking binge and on a fifteen year old girl.

Santos does not return and, within two months, Lourdes is forced to give up her apartment and car. She rents a garage for $300 a month, where she and Diana share a mattress on the floor. The garage roof leaks, and slugs crawl onto their mattress. Diana grows ill, but Lourdes cannot afford medicine.

Lourdes becomes a *fichera*, a type of prostitute who gets bar patrons to spend money on drinks. Nine months later, she finds work cleaning offices and houses by day, and work at a gas station by night. She works ten hour shifts, and then picks up Diana from school and drops her off at a babysitter's house. Lourdes sleeps one or two hours, then returns to work until two o'clock in the morning. She takes side jobs, working at a candy factory for $2.25 an hour. Lourdes is able to send money to Enrique and Belky again.

Furious about the new baby, Belky withdraws emotionally from her mother. When he can talk to her on the phone, Enrique continues to ask when she will return home. Around this time, Enrique has the idea to travel north in search of her. Meanwhile, Lourdes wants to become an American citizen and legally bring her children to the country. Unfortunately, she spends $3,850 on fraudulent storefront immigration counselors who steal her money.

One year, Lourdes promises to come home by Christmas. Enrique waits by the front door for her, but she never arrives. He asks his grandmother how Lourdes got to the United States and she replies "maybe…she went on the trains" (19).

Lourdes is afraid that returning to Honduras will prohibit her from ever returning to the U.S. She fears the smugglers (called coyotes) who are often alcoholics or drug addicts. Lourdes knows all too well of the dangers. One of her friends had paid a smuggler to bring her sister to Long Beach, California. In Mexico, the sister and others were put in a overloaded boat which capsized and killed most of them. They were buried in a shallow grave on the beach.

Children face particular danger if entrusted to smugglers. They are often abandoned and left to the care of the foster homes in Mexico or the United States. Pictures of these children are broadcast over the television in the hopes that someone will recognize them and bring them home again. Smugglers charge up to $3,000 per child, and sometimes as high as $6,000. To bring a child over by commercial air costs $10,000, and Lourdes does not have enough money to send for even one of her children.

In Honduras, Enrique begins to rebel. He hits other children and is suspended from school three times, though he does eventually complete elementary school. Now fourteen years old, he spends most of his time on the streets of Carrizal, playing soccer and refusing to sell spices. His grandmother beats him with a belt, but Enrique continues to misbehave. Upset but determined, Marìa Marcos asks Lourdes by letter to find Enrique a new home, since she is too old to take care of a rebellious youth. Lourdes arranges for Enrique to stay with her brother, Marco. Enrique likes the new arrangement and developments a strong relationship with his uncle.

A year passes, and Lourdes moves to North Carolina to work as a waitress in a Mexican restaurant. Away from the big city, she can save more money to hopefully bring her children to the U.S. She meets a house painter from Honduras, and they soon fall in love.

Enrique begins working for his uncle, washing cars and changing money on the Honduran border. Tragically, Marco and his brother Victor are killed during an exchange. To pay for their funerals, Lourdes sends all of the money she had saved to bring her children to America. Within days of Marco's funeral, Enrique is forced out on the streets by his uncle's girlfriend, who has no use for him.

Enrique next stays with his maternal grandmother, who shares her house with two of his aunts and four of his cousins. Enrique descends into a deep depression, and becomes introverted. He misses Marco terribly, and drops out of school. He begins to sniff glue, until his grandmother throws him out of the house. He is forced to live in a stone hut on their property; it has no electricity.

Soon after Marco's funeral, Enrique meets and falls in love with María Isabel, who has also been shuffled from home to home during her youth. Enrique wants to have a child with María Isabel, so that they can start a family together and he will therefore never feel alone or abandoned again. Regrettably, Enrique develops a worse drug habit, sniffing glue from baby jars and smoking marijuana. His family tries to intervene, but he continues to spiral out of control. Enrique begins to hallucinate - he does not recognize his family, and once tries to throw himself off a hill. The family chooses not to tell Lourdes of his condition.

On his sixteenth birthday, Enrique makes his first attempt to ride atop the trains. He and his friend Jóse leave Honduras on a bus headed to Guatemala, which is near the Mexican border. They eventually cross into Mexico and board a freight train, but are robbed by police officers and then arrested. They are released, and then board another train. For the first time, Enrique jumps from car to car on the slow-moving train. He slips and falls, but luckily lands onto a padded surface. They are caught near Tierra Blanca in Veracruz, and again deported. He and Jóse sell coconuts for bus fare, and then return home.

Enrique sinks deeper into drugs, until he owes 6,000 *lempiras* (about $400) to his dealer. He does not have the money. The dealer threatens to kill his cousin if Enrique does not pay up. In desperation, Enrique steals jewelry from his Rosa Amalia, who then reports him to the police. When confronted, Enrique claims he was too high to know what he was doing, and warns the family that his cousin is in danger. Enrique's uncle then gets him a job at a tire store, where he earns $15 a week. Despite the pleas of both his family and Marìa Isabel, Enrique continues to use drugs. One day, he gets into a heated argument with his aunt, and hits her in the buttocks. His grandmother kicks him off of her property.

Marìa Isabel is urged to leave Enrique, but she loves him and thinks she is pregnant with his child. Enrique believes the only person who can help him is his mother, but he has no money for a smuggler, and he dreads leaving Marìa Isabel behind. Nevertheless, Enrique finally sells his belongings and says goodbye to his family and girlfriend. On March 2, 2000, with only $57, a change of clothes, and his mother's phone number written on a scrap of paper and inside of the waistband of his jeans, Enrique sets out for the United States.

Analysis

Enrique's Journey opens with a photo of a young Enrique looking sadly into the camera while wearing his kindergarten graduation gown and hat. His expression is somber, which sets the tone for the first few sections of the book, in which a young Enrique adjusts to life without his mother. It also implicitly establishes one of Nazario's main purposes: to consider how a child copes with harsh realities, of both poverty and perceived abandonment.

The chapter *The Boy Left Behind* includes many of the book's central themes - abandonment, family, and love. Lourdes has made the fateful decision to go to the United States to seek work so that she might send money, food, and clothing back to her two young children in Honduras. However, this decision has a myriad of consequences. What Nazario is most interested in here are the emotional consequences. Both Lourdes and the children must combat feelings of guilt and shame because of what poverty has led her to do. The book is powerful partly because it neither judges nor justifies Lourdes. Both potential decisions - to leave or to stay - can lead to terrible and heartbreaking consequences. Nazario is content to explore the issue, and to present both sides of the argument, and how each impacts family, love, and feelings of abandonment.

Enrique is established here as a protagonist, which is interesting considering that the book is primarily a work of journalism rather than fiction. However, it is an effective choice to set him up as a character with a clearly established goal. It creates a dramatic momentum summarized in the final question of the prologue, and which leads a reader to root for him as he undertakes this journey. While Nazario's book is based on reality and documented interviews, she nevertheless structures it with a dramatic shape - the character is put into a difficult situation in this opening chapter, and he decides to undertake a journey to improve his life.

The imagery in this chapter is striking. Lourdes's poverty is drawn with a myriad of specific details - for instance, at one point she sits next to a Pizza Hut, an American food chain, while Enrique rides a broomstick, pretending it's a donkey. Marìa Marco's home, a shack of wooden slats that she built herself, with no running water and little electricity, exemplifies not only the theme of poverty, but its visceral nature. Nazario's strength as a journalist serves her well as she establishes the reality of the challenges these families face.

Ironically, Lourdes's commitment to family produces a disintegration of the family. It is more than just her absence. Enrique's father leaves him to start another family, and both Enrique and Belky must confront their feelings of abandonment. Whereas Belky is able to compartmentalize and turn emotionally from her mother, Enrique seems to idealize her even as his emotional scars lead him to bad, harmful behavior. His disrepect towards the family that takes care of him only emphasizes how Lourdes's attempt to be a strong mother have in some ways hurt her son.

Nazario also explores the irony of the American promise. Symbols of the American dream - Disneyland's magic castle, the lights of Los Vegas, the size of New York City - flutter in the background of Lourdes's mind as she travels to the United States. The reality she faces is markedly different. Los Angeles is full of cruelty and poverty, all of which bite particularly hard since they are forced reminders of what she has left behind. And yet she *is* able to make money by embracing these aspects of American society. Again, Nazario makes no easy attacks, but is content to explore the irony of both sides.

The details on smugglers are particularly intriguing. Firstly, they are clearly expensive, a particular challenge considering their customers tend to be poverty stricken. Secondly, smugglers, especially those who traffic in children, are notoriously cruel, according to the United States Border Patrol. Smugglers, who often drink or use drugs on the journey, have been known to rape their charges, to leave them in the desert, at bus stations, or at the first sign of danger. Children who are abandoned by their smugglers now face the world alone; some die of exposure while others, luckily, are picked up by immigration officials and are taken to shelters. Although not an ideal situation, they are at leat safe.

Enrique's rebellion towards the end of the section provides the most in-depth manifestation of the abandonment theme. He is not only rebellious, but also mean. He makes a teacher cry, and hits other children. When he finally does turn inward, he is cruel to himself through his glue-sniffing. This behavior isolates him from others, and leaves him feeling that nobody loves him. His only possible reprieve is the mother he had idealized, the mother who the reader knows faces her own challenges. Though he leaves his girlfriend - who he believes might be pregnant with his child - it is clear that staying in Honduras will likely mean his end, whether by arrest or death. His journey has begun.

Summary and Analysis of Seeking Mercy

Summary

Near a small rail side town in the state of Oaxaca, Mexico, Enrique hobbles up towards a field hand. He is severely beaten, and dressed only in his underwear. The field hand gives him clothes and water, while women from the town give him money. A mayor from a neighboring town arrives in a pickup truck, and takes Enrique to a local hospital. Though the task irks him, the mayor knows it costs more to bury a dead migrant than to pay the $60 county fee to have him treated by a doctor. The mayor has already buried eight migrants in the last eighteen months.

Enrique agrees to go to the hospital, but recoils when he sees the mayor's driver, whom he recognizes as someone who robbed him the day before. Nazario explains that the Mexican judicial police routinely stop trains in order to rob and beat migrants. Corrupt police have even been known to kidnap migrants, and hold them for ransom from family in the United States.

Nazario rewinds her narrative to explain how Enrique ended up here. Enrique has now made six attempts to cross through Mexico towards the United States. His first attempt was explained in the previous section - he and his friend Jóse were apprehended by *la migra* (Mexican immigration authorities) after thirty-one days of travel and then deported on what they call the *El Bus de Lágrimos* (Bus of Tears). Over 100,000 migrants ride this bus annually when being returned to the border with Guatemala.

On his second attempt, Enrique was caught on the trains and deported. His third attempt was ceded after only two days in Mexico. On his fourth attempt, he was caught sleeping on top of a mausoleum in a graveyard.

His fifth attempt was also short lived - he was caught only a week into his journey. His sixth was almost successful. Enrique traveled 1,564 miles to reach the Rio Grande, which marks the border between Mexico and the U.S. He was eating alone next to the railroad tracks when *la migra* found him and sent him to a Mexican detention center called El Corralón.

Each time he is deported, Enrique knows he must quickly reenter Mexico to avoid the dangers of the lawless Guatemalan border towns. Enrique prefers to cross the river in El Carmen, which he does on his seventh attempt. He reaches the trains and begins to ride, but is soon attacked by six men at night. They rob him of his clothes and money, and savagely beat him.

One of the men strangles him with the sleeve of a jacket, while another beats him with a club. As he is being accosted, Enrique sees the slip of paper with his mother's number flutter away. When the man strangling him slips, Enrique stands quickly and flees them, jumping from the top of the train to a lower level, and then off the train altogether. He crawls to the safety of a mango tree, where he sleeps for twelve hours.

Enrique is taken to a medical facility, where his injuries are treated. His left eye lid is damaged and may never recover. His back is bruised, and there are several lesions on his right leg. Three teeth are broken, and he has an open wound on his head. The doctor tells Enrique that he is lucky. Every month, ten migrants fall from the train or are beaten by gangsters and are then treated at this facility. Other migrants are mutilated by the train, losing their limbs in the process.

Enrique leaves the hospital after one day of care. As he hobbles down the street, headed back to the trains, men and women give him *pesos* out of pity. Enrique flags down a car and asks for a ride, but the driver proves to be an immigration officer and Enrique soon finds himself on the bus back to Guatemala. Although he has failed again, Enrique remains determined to reach the United States.

Back in Honduras, María Isabel waits for Enrique to return. She blames herself for his departure and grows thin and ill, wondering whether she is really pregnant. María Isabel quits her job and decides to also brave the journey north with a friend, in search of Enrique.

Analysis

Cruelty and suffering are underlying motifs of the story, and are particularly notable in this chapter. The cruelty of the gangsters, the bandits, *la migra*, and others are recognized by the migrants, even though they discuss these issues in hushed tones. Not only do they need to fear these forces, but they also have to fear retaliation if they complain too loudly. Their bodies and spirits are battered by this journey, and ultimately, they are alone for its duration. Any friends made on the trip could betray them or get lost on the journey. And if injured, a migrant might fall by the wayside and not be found for days.

One might expect a work of this sort to focus on institutions, but Nazario gives equal focus to the bandits who exploit the migration trend for their own benefit. She uses great detail in describing the attack upon Enrique, and notes that the men would have killed him even after robbing him had he not escaped. Their violence and cruelty is unjustified, and reflects darker impulses than simply greed and poverty. Perhaps the most upsetting fact about Enrique's attack is what he learns in the clinic: he should consider himself lucky, since many would have died in his circumstances.

When Central American migrants are injured in Mexico, they have no recourse but charity. They recover at the mercy of the hospitals or the Red Cross, all of which is a problem because of limited resources. These institutions often lack necessary funds, medicine, or trained physicians to properly treat the extensive injury the migrants suffer. Some, even those who have lost limbs, are released from the hospital much too soon. Enrique is evidence of this. There are also private institutions - one example Nazario will later explore is The Shelter of Jesus the Good Shepherd, run by Olga Sánchez Martinez.

The suffering and deaths of these migrants are commemorated along the railways by a plethora of border art. A form of activism, the art usually includes images of the cross, which symbolize martyrdom and death. More political messages attacking immigration authorities and corrupt police are painted across coffins, along walls, and even on the trains. Border art murals extend as far inland as California. In many ways, the art also gives a voice to these many immigrant who die alone, and have little recourse to individuality while struggling through this journey. Their trek requires them to be alone for its duration, and so small gestures like this art attempt to remind them that their lives are being acknowledged.

Enrique continues to be a protagonist with which the reader can empathize. Certainly, he is not perfect, as his behavior in Honduras revealed, but he shows his heroic perseverance in this chapter. Despite his injuries and the daunting prospect of having to attempt the journey for the eighth time, Enrique maintains hope of his success. Hope, a dominant theme within the text, serves Enrique well. Even while aboard the Bus of Tears - a name with clear symbolic quality - he declares he will not give up. His last ride on the Bus of Tears serves as a type of a climax to this first act of the story - our protagonist has faced a severe beating, but recommits himself. Even tears cannot stop him. He must go it alone, but he is ready for that.

Despite his injuries, or perhaps because of them, he feels more determined than ever to get to the United States. Many migrants express their desire to persevere despite overwhelming odds, which characterizes the true extent of their suffering back home.

Summary and Analysis of Facing the Beast

Summary

Enrique wades through the Rio Suchiate toward Mexico, into the southern state of Chiapas, which migrants call *la bestia* ("the beast"). Seventeen year old Enrique knows what he will face in Chiapas: bandits will try to rob him, police will try to deport him, and gangs may kill him. It is the hardest single section of the journey. Despite the risks, Enrique pushes on.

Once he crosses the river, he spends the night in a cemetery, on top of a mausoleum to avoid the police. From here, he can easily hear the trains. It is important that he catch the first train he hears, since it might be several days until another passes. Under the protection of the Mara Salvatrucha gang, Enrique befriends a young man named Big Daddy. That night, they are both apprehended during a police raid and taken to a holding cell. Other migrants help him escape over the wall, and he returns to the cemetery to wait for a 10:00am train.

When he hears the first rumblings of the train, the cemetery around him comes to life - dozens of migrants appear from behind bushes, trees, and tombs, and all race toward the train, positioning themselves to grab onto one of its many ladders. As the train rushes past at 20 miles per hour, Enrique hoists himself up onto a hopper car.

There, he encounters an eleven year old boy who is also traveling to the Untied State to see his mother. According to the Grupo Beta, a government sponsored migrants right group, about 20%-30% of the migrants who board the trains in Tapachula are under the age of fifteen.

Enrique considers where he should hide on the train. The boxcars are dangerous, as there is little to hold on to, but *la migra* does not normally go up there. Inside the boxcars is worse. He could be trapped inside for days, without food or water, and die of heat exhaustion. He could hide under the cars, between the axles, but he has grown too big to fit safely. Enrique decides to settle in on top of the hopper car, and holds on for dear life. He is afraid his car will tip over.

The train begins to slow as they reach La Arrocera, a strict immigration checkpoint. Enrique fears La Arrocera; it is isolated and he is too exposed on top of the train. The other migrants begin to yell warnings. *La migra* is here, so Enrique jumps from car to car, finally landing on a boxcar. *La migra* spots him and demands he come down, even throwing rocks to force him, but he refuses. Instead, he jumps from the train into some bushes. He hears gunshots behind him.

Now, a new danger awaits him. *Madrinas* are men who wear civilian clothing but help the authorities capture migrants. The worst crimes against migrants, rape and torture, are attributed to *madrinas*. Sometimes *madrians* ride the tops of trains and count the number of migrants on board so they can radio ahead to the checkpoints. Even if he can avoid them, he must contend with electrified wires as he attempts to bypass the checkpoint and reboard the train.

The other major threat in La Arrocera is bandits who patrol the area, ready to rob migrants of their money and clothes. The locals are terrified of the bandits and will never testify against them in court. Similarly, the police turn a blind eye to their activities. There is a red brick house near the checkpoint where bandits often rape and kill young women. Nazario states that one in six migrant women are sexually assaulted during their journey north, according to a 1997 University of Houston study. To protect themselves, some women cut off their hair and strap down their breasts, pretending to be boys, while others write the words “Tengo Sida" ("I have AIDS") across their chest.

Enrique reaches the Cuil bridge, one of the most dangerous places on the journey north because ruthless bandits lay in wait for migrants there. Enrique makes it across unharmed. He has survived La Arrocera.

Desperate for water, Enrique approaches a nearby house. He knows that the Mexicans of Chiapas barely tolerate Central American migrants, and consider them ignorant and poor. They believe Central Americans bring disease, prostitution, and crime to the area, and take away jobs from Mexicans. Boys like Enrique are often turned away when they beg for food or water. This time, though, Enrique is lucky; he finds a nice woman who gives him water, bread, and beans. Enrique suddenly hears the horn of the train and soon reboards a hopper.

It is 105 degrees, and Enrique's palms burn as he holds tight to the hopper, standing on the narrow ledge of the fuel tanker just inches from the wheels. The heat saps his energy, but he cannot allow himself to fall asleep, since it could mean death. Some migrants strap themselves to the train with belts or t-shirts, while others nap on the tracks, waiting for the next train. Both alternatives often leave migrants mangled or killed.

Falling asleep also makes one potential prey for the Mara Salvatrucha (MA) gangsters, who roam the train tops looking for "sleepers" (83). This gang will rob migrants mercilessly, knowing the migrants will never press charges, and have little recourse to escape while the train barrels along. Some pretend to be migrants themselves, so they can determine who has money or food. They are usually on drugs, either marijuana or crack cocaine. Migrants who resist are tossed overboard or beaten with a variety of weapons. MA gang members have skulls tattooed on their ankles, which indicate the number of people they have killed. Their ruthlessness is well known. Once, they allegedly threw a man from a train and then forced two boys to have sex with one another.

Enrique is fortunate to have befriended El Brujo, a Mara Salvatrucha member. Although not a member himself, Enrique has been protected by association because of his friendship with El Brujo. However, recently, he refused to help the MS gang get revenge on the 18th Street gang. Since then, he has been alone on the trains, and is a frequent victim of beatings by MS members.

To keep himself awake, Enrique jumps from car to car, allowing his fear to fuel his adrenaline. Other migrants take amphetamines, slap themselves, exercise, talk to one another, or sing. Soon, the night passes and Chiapas is behind him. Although Enrique knows he has a long way to go, he is proud of himself for having made it past "the beast."

Most of the migrants who had set out with Enrique have been caught, deported, killed by the trains, or felled by gangsters. The Red Cross estimates that nearly one migrant every other day loses a limb to the train. This does not include the many migrants who have been decapitated or cut in half by the trains. If a Central American migrant dies, they usually do not carry ID and are lowered unnamed into a mass grave.

Those who have lost limbs are treated by the Red Cross. However, if they are near Tapachula, they go to the Shelter of Jesus the Good Shepherd. There, Olga Sánchez Martínez tries to heal them. "No one tells me something can't be done. Everything can be cured. Nothing is impossible," Olga says (90). Nazario tells Olga's story. Olga suffered many indignities in her life, including cancer, after which she promised to devote her life to healing others if God would heal her. Ten years later, she remains committed to healing migrants. She brings them into her own home, founded a shelter for them, dresses their wounds, and attempts to lift their spirits. To finance her operation, she begs for donations, seeking thousands of dollars a week to buy prosthetic limbs for the migrants. Olga works for free, seven days a week, and has not had a serious illness since her promise to God.

As Enrique enters the state of Oaxaca, he disembarks the train to recoup. It is crucial to blend in to the Mexican background so as to avoid deportation. He removes his dirty yellow shirt and replaces it with a white one. He washes his arms in the stream and spends what little money he has on a haircut so he will not stick out. Most Mexicans have straight dark hair, while Central Americans tend to have curlier hair. To further blend in, Enrique must also alter his speech and word choice. For instance, *agua* means water in Mexico, but means soda in Honduras. Also, he must remember that Mexican weigh items in kilograms instead of pounds. Migrants also remove Central American tags from their clothing, or wear Mexican sports team memorabilia. Nazario gives many details of how Central Americans attempt to disguise their identity while recouping here.

Back in Honduras, María Isabel is persuaded by her family to stay at home. She fears for Enrique, but agrees with her mother that the dangers of traveling north far outweigh the potential benefits. She is still uncertain whether she is pregnant, and is worried that the journey could cause complications if she is.

Analysis

Enrique's eighth attempt to go north begins at a river, the Rìo Suchiate in Guatemala. The rivers in *Enrique's Journey* serve as symbols of renewal. Each time Enrique crosses a river, he is entering a new phase of his travel. When he finally crosses the Rio Grande, it serves as his baptism into a new phase of his life. However, at this point, he faces the Rìo Suchiate, across which lies Chiapas, "the beast." If the Rio Grande offers salvation, the Rìo Suchiate threatens damnation. Wearing a cap which appropriately reads "No Fear," he bravely presses on and accepts the challenge.

The scene in the cemetery, when Enrique is caught by police, illustrates an interesting juxtaposition within the story. The migrants lay on top of graves, near not only the dead but also near sites of frequent rape, attack, and murder. The migrants themselves are hunted like animals, and their deaths are sometimes undocumented, as if they had never existed at all - many are buried in mass unmarked graves. It is ironic that they should find solace and peace in a place of death when their own fates are so uncertain. They cannot even count on a dignified death, a point which must resonate for them while awaiting the train in a cemetery. However, the irony only stresses how high the stakes are for these migrants. They must accept these unfortunate ironies as part of their burden if they are to arrive at their destinations.

The train itself also serves as something of a symbol for the journey, both because it offers promise and because of its many dangers. The boxcar, as Enrique explains, is a closed container that holds cargo. When not in use, the boxcar resembles a large empty box. Nazario interviewed a migrant who had been placed inside a boxcar with forty others by their smuggler. The doors were shut and the container soon became an oven in the 100 degree weather. Several people died. It is easy to become trapped inside the boxcar, and they are also one of the first cars to be searched by *la migra*. The fact that this ostensibly most comfortable spot is also fraught with dangers exemplifies the contradictory nature of the train. The tops of boxcars are very unsafe, but are less frequently searched. Hoppers are usually large, open containers that carry bulk cargo like grain, sugar, fertilizer, or coal. They are lower to the ground than boxcars, and hence more often searched, but they are easier to access. The choice of car is very important and can help migrants survive, but with each decision a migrant must play the odds. In a sense, the decision is almost arbitrary considering how many factors are out of their control, but the decision must be made nevertheless.

However, the train also serves as a symbol of hope and faith. Certainly, these migrants have a deep religious faith from their culture, but their faith on this journey is more palpable - they believe they can brave the dangerous journey to make it north. The train is essential towards reaching that goal. One can determine a migrant's outlook by which name he or she uses to name the train. Some call it *El Tren de la Muerte* (Train of Death) or *El Tran Devorador* (The Train That Devours), both of which speak to its destructive potential. Others call it *El Tren Peregrino* (The Pilgrim's Train), which reflects its spiritual quality. Enrique prefers to call the train *El Caballo de Hierro* (the Iron Horse). What he recognizes is not its spiritual potential but rather its physical strength. It reflects his persistence and determination, his belief that he will succeed through force of will.

Summary and Analysis of Gifts and Faith

Summary

A statue of Jesus Christ welcomes Enrique to Veracruz. It is April 2000, and Enrique has made it one-third of the way through Mexico. Many of his fellow migrants attribute their success to God. They have prayed for guidance and protection, and carry their Bibles wrapped in plastic as a source of validation. They relate particularly to the Twenty-Third Psalm, which reads, "Yea, though I walk through the valley of the shadow of death, I will fear no evil: for thou art with me; thy rod and thy staff they comfort me." Enrique does not ask God for help, as he believes he has committed too many sins. He expects the worst, but is surprised by the reward he receives in Veracruz and Oaxaca.

Unlike the people of Chiapas, those of Veracruz and Oaxaca are friendly toward migrants. They shout to signal if police are nearby, giving the migrants time to react. Women and children run along the sides of the train with small bundles, which they throw up as gifts. Enrique receives several loaves of bread from woman and a boy. He is overwhelmed by their generosity.

In fact, residents of Veracruz are known for their kindness. One migrant says, "We could never keep going forward without people like this" (104-105). Although poor themselves, the townspeople give sweaters, clothes, bread, water, lemonade, and more to the migrants as they pass on the trains. Marìa Luisa Mora Martin is over a hundred years old, but she and her daughter regularly throw bags of food and supplies to migrants.

In interviews with Nazario, the residents provide their philosophies on kindness. One person says, "I don't like to feel that I have eaten and they haven't" (105). Others say it is rewarding to help the suffering migrants. They are all encouraged to give by the local bishop, Hipólito Reyes Larios, who quotes the Gospel of Matthew to encourage mercy and compassion for strangers. Local priests, in individual towns, also compare the journey of the migrants to that of the baby Jesus as his family fled from Israel.

The Church is also active in protecting migrants from police abuse in Veracruz. Nazario tells how migrants often claim sanctuary in churches, and how priests facilitate releases if they are arrested nearby. One town turned its church into a permanent sanctuary and shelter. Another church, Maria Auxiliadora, allows migrants to stay in the courtyard where they are served daily meals. For over two decades, the church members and priests of Veracruz have fought for the rights of the migrants, holding public protests outside of any hospital that allows *la migra* to deport injured migrants before they are healed.

Individual citizens also offer protection to migrants. Some residents offer migrants protection from the police by allowing them to stay in their homes or hide in their gardens and backyards. The police have threatened to arrest church members who aid the migrants; some have even been charged and released only after paying thousands of *pesos*. Though the police respect the sanctuary of church grounds, individual citizens are liable to smuggling charges for housing migrants.

Whole communities have stood up to police abuses. Nazario tells of an incident in 2000 when drunk police shot at migrants who had left the train, sending them fleeing into the hills. In the chase, a young, pregnant woman was shot in the arm. The police chased her up the mountain, where he beat and kicked her until she collapsed. The townspeople then confronted the police, and chased them away. Afterwards, a local man was found dead, presumably having been shot in the confusion. The next day, five hundred residents of different towns marched to city hall in Nogales to demand retribution for the man's death, and the release of any migrants arrested in the raid. Eight police officers were fired over the incident.

As Enrique departs Veracruz on another train, he befriends two boys going to America - one is seventeen, the other thirteen. He relishes their companionship. Soon, they arrive in Mexico City, where all hospitality vanishes. People are hostile here, on edge. Churches hire armed guards to stand watch during mass so that parishioners are not robbed. The attitude toward migrants is the opposite of that in Veracruz. One woman tells of a local man who was beaten, robbed, and raped by migrants. As a result of this fear, people in Mexico City offer little charity.

Enrique begs for food, but finds only one woman willing to give him any. He then hides in a three-foot-wide concrete culvert in a field just north of the station. There, he times the arrival of a 10:30am northbound train to the Texas border. He and his two friends board the train and find room in a boxcar as they travel away from Mexico City. Enrique sleeps well, but is eventually awakened by police officers who escort the boys from the train. Instead of deporting them, however, the police take them to their *jefe* (boss), who feeds them and gives them toothpaste. The *jefe* warns them to leave the train before the next security guard station, which is notoriously harsh.

Before they board the next train, Enrique decides to find a job. He does not want to arrive in the U.S. penniless. He works for a bricklayer and earn 80 *pesos*, shoes, and clothing. His employer tells him to take a *combi* (minibus) through the next checkpoint, since vans are not searched by *la migra*. He is then advised to take a bus to Matehuala, where he may be able to hitchhike on a truck up to the Rio Grande. Enrique follows the advice, and soon arrives in Matehuala, where a kind truck driver gives him a ride. As they near the Rio Grande, the driver tells the police officers at Los Pocitos checkpoint that Enrique is his assistant, and they do not question him.

The driver drops Enrique off in Nuevo Laredo, and Enrique uses most of his money to take a bus into the heart of the city. There, he meets a Honduran man who takes him to an encampment near the Rio Grande. Here, Enrique can see the United States. He feels overwhelmed, having spent forty-six days traveling, but the proximity reminds him of how much emotional distance remains between him and his mother, and he admits a sadness mixed in his excitement.

Analysis

A statue of Jesus Christ greets Enrique and others as their train enters Veracruz. It is a symbol of the unexpected charity that the migrants will receive. When Enrique sees a woman and a boy running alongside the tracks, he fears they will throw rocks. Such pessimism makes sense, considering his negative experiences so far in Mexico. So when the family throws not rocks but gifts, they give him more than food; they give him hope.

Hope, a recurring theme throughout the text, is most apparent in this chapter. The status of Jesus Christ, a universal symbol of faith and hope, opens the door for an abundance of charity from the men and women of Veracruz. Although Enrique does not believe he is worthy of God's goodness (a result of his abandonment issues and guilt over his own sins), many of the migrants are bolstered by their Christian faith. They pray together, or read psalms like the Ninety-first, which reads, "There shall no evil befall thee, neither shall any plague come nigh thy dwelling. For he shall give his angels charge over thee, to keep thee in all thy ways." Another favorite prayer of the migrants is *La Oració a las Tres Divinas Personas*, which is a prayer to the Holy Trinity that asks for guidance from the saints.

Whether the kindness of Veracruz is inspired by prayer or not, it is undeniably a selfless charity. After all, the most a person can expect for his or her gift is a quick 'thanks' as the train continues to rush by. Though these people are extremely poor - Nazario goes into detail in describing their poverty - they are nevertheless moved by the suffering of those who have less than them.

Nazario also indicates that their kindness is inspired by a particular bishop, and the local priests under him. This is one of many indications in the book of individuals who inspire great kindness by fostering institutions devoted to charity. Nazario's book is unique in refusing to offer easy solutions to the immigration problem and its complicated institutions, but she does often implicitly suggest that individuals can make a large difference by basing institutions around their own kindness. Olga, in the previous chapter, is another example.

Mexico City is the opposite of Veracruz. Hope is difficult to justify here. Enrique does meet one woman who is willing to share her food with him, but only after many others have turned him down. Suffering, a continuing motif, is evident in many ways in the Mexico City section. Firstly, Nazario points out that Enrique continues to harbor scars from his terrible beating weeks before. There is a suggestion that he is given charity sometimes because his appearance inspires pity. Secondly, Nazario does not judge the residents of Mexico City for their animosity, but instead suggests that they confront their own suffering. Mexico City is one of the most violent cities in the country. Migrants have not necessarily been kind to residents there, both in terms of the economy and safety. Hence, they are reticent to be too open.

Kindness, an uncommon theme in the text, is found in unlikely places for Enrique. Some examples are the *jefe* who helps him, the bricklayer who hires him, and the truck driver who gives him a ride. Kindness translates to hope through the friends Enrique makes on the train. At this point, the number of migrants has dwindled since so many have been captured or killed, and so intimacy is easier to achieve. This happens with the young boys, and the three share food, conversation, and solace. Although they do not travel together for very long, this brief moment of normalcy and companionship helps to bolster Enrique's spirit. Like the bread that he received in Veracruz, his friendship with the two boys enables him to push forward to the final great challenge: crossing the Rio Grande into the United States.

Summary and Analysis of On the Border

Summary

An American Border Patrol agent yells into his bullhorn, "You are in American territory. Turn back. Thank you for returning to your country" (137). Enrique is stymied. He has been in Nuevo Laredo, living in an encampment on the banks of the Rio Grande, for days. He has no idea if is mother is still in North Carolina. He does not have her phone number or enough money to call her. He knows his mother must have learned from relatives that he is gone. He decides to earn money to buy phone cards, so that he can call his former employer in Honduras (he remembers that number), to try and obtain his mother's number. Each card costs fifty *pesos* each; he decides to wash cars to earn it.

Enrique stays at an encampment for migrants, coyotes, drug addicts, and criminals. It is hidden from the U.S. immigration authorities by high reeds, thereby enabling the migrants to watch the agents and their sports utility vehicles. Enrique knows he will have to cross the river in order to get to the U.S., but so far has no idea how to achieve this. Some migrants swim over, while others use inner tubes.

Each evening, Enrique takes a bucket and two rags to a popular taco stand. There, he attracts potential costumers with a red rag. He earns very little money. Luckily, two local parish centers offer free meals to migrants. Though overcrowded, Enrique benefits from the charity, and meets other children who have similar stories to his own.

The encampment is run by a man called El Tiríndaro, a *patero* who smuggles people into the U.S. by pushing them across the river in an inner tube. He is a heroin addict who finances his drug use through tattooing people, petty theft, and smuggling. In Mexico, heroin is called *la cura* (the cure).

Enrique, known in the encampment as *El Hongo* (the mushroom) because of his shyness, continues to explore options as he lives under the protection of El Tiríndaro, who considers him a potential customer for smuggling. For $1,200, El Tiríndaro can not only get a migrant across the river, but also set him up with a smuggling operation that will get him further into the country. Luckily, many migrants in the camp look after him because of his age, which allows him to explore options. Each night, when he leaves to wash cars, he is scared to be outside of their protection.

Unfortunately, Enrique is not making enough money for phone cards, and feels guilty when he uses his meager savings on food. El Tiríndaro helps Enrique by taking him to sell the clothing left behind on the riverbank by migrants. Finally, Enrique saves enough to buy two phone cards. To celebrate, he gets a tattoo which reads "EnriqueLourdes" across his chest. He knows his mother will not be pleased. The next day, hungry, he trades one of his phone cards for money to buy food. He begins to sniff glue again, to battle his hunger, fear, and loneliness. Then, someone steals his washing bucket, and he must beg to make money for another phone card.

Enrique considers crossing the river by himself, but he cannot swim and if he were caught, he would be deported. Trains going from Mexico into Texas are out of the question, as they are searched several times and scanned with infrared telescopes to sense body heat. He also cannot walk through Texas, as he is unfamiliar with the terrain. Migrants have been known to die of dehydration in 120 degree weather, or to end up shot by Texan ranchers.

Nazario discusses the extent of security at the border. The INS has hired 5,600 additional agents since 1993 to staff the border. Some agents can track the footprints of migrants as they walk through the Texas desert. Others can tell how old the footprints are and in which directions the migrants are headed. Agents are paid to bring migrants in, and are given a bonus for catching them. They also insist that they actually work in the best interest of migrants, since migrants are too often wounded or killed by rattlesnake bites, train injuries, dehydration, or animals like coyotes and bobcats. In the depressing, difficult terrain, many migrants are thankful when apprehended.

Enrique decides to hire a smuggler, and chooses El Tiríndaro because of his high success rate. Before he can call his family in Honduras, someone steals his right shoe in the middle of the night. Enrique is furious; shoes are almost as important as food in the encampment. He has gone through seven pairs during his journey north. Desperately, he searches for a shoe and finds one on the riverbank - unfortunately, it is a left show, and so now he has wears two left shoes.

On May 19th, Enrique visits Padre Leo, a local priest and advocate for migrant care. Padre Leo is a disheveled but lovable man who rides a blue bicycle. Migrants call him their "champion" because he literally gives them the shirt off his back and the shoes from his feet (175). He also allows the migrants to use the church phone, which Enrique does to call his old boss, who eventually connects him with his relatives, who in turn give him Lourdes's phone number. He next calls Lourdes collect, and they begin preparations to hire a coyote for $1,200.

Analysis

From the banks of the Rio Grande, the overwhelming sight of the United States represents not only the illusive imagery of the American dream, but also the culmination of Enrique's journey. His mother feels nearby, although he has no idea whether she is still in North Carolina and has no way to reach her. The promise of the U.S. stands in stark contrast to to the harsh poverty of Nuevo Laredo, where Enrique thanklessly washes cars but can barely save anything.

One of the photographs by Don Bartletti, included in *Enrique's Journey*, shows Enrique washing cars at night. Nazario first met Enrique in Nuevo Lardeo during this time period. Her personal insight into the encampment, the stories of other child migrants, and the information she relates about the U.S. Border Patrol all work together to provide a well rounded and insightful image of what life is like for Enrique without compromising the narrative. Bartletti's photographs further enhance the overall story, giving faces to the names, which naturally underscores the reality of Enrique's situation.

Nazario's authorial interjections do not detract from Enrique's position as a protagonist. It is an exciting development from a narrative standpoint - our hero has almost reached his goal, but suddenly finds himself facing a new set of overwhelming odds. We continue to root for him, even as setbacks like losing a shoe make his success seem impossible. The chapter ends with something of a cliffhanger - he will get the money! - but clearly, there are more challenges to face.

The phone cards serve as physical representations of Enrique's hope. When he trades one of them for food, it is a visceral reminder of the poverty that grounds him even at his strongest. Were he to fail now, he would have to start over for a ninth time. Two symbols are juxtaposed in this section to exhibit his conflict - his tattoo expresses his unshakeable hope, while the phone card, which he sells the next day, represents the inescapable demands of money and food. These are the forces that compete throughout the story, and no matter how close he gets, the conflict continue to resonate.

Other mothers in the encampment are less enthusiastic or hopeful. As Mother's Day passes, the young women Nazario speaks to relate how worried they are for the children they have left behind. Mother's Day is a harsh reminder of the distance between themselves and their children. These mothers pray for their children's safety, too. One mother says she fears she will lose the love of her children if she stays too long in the United States. On the other side of the Rio Grande, Lourdes worries for her son and prays to St. Judas, patron saint of those in need as well as those who are lost.

Drug use, a distressing but dominant motif within the text, reappears at the end of "On the Border" when Enrique begins to sniff glue again. What is heartbreaking is that we understand the forces that lead him in that direction - his fear, his hunger, his loneliness - but also know that such activity could compromise his mission. His love for her has not faltered, but it now competes with his more physical pain. Narratively, the book stays intriguing as we wonder not only whether Enrique will make it to the U.S., but also whether he will be able to find personal happiness there.

Summary and Analysis of A Dark River, Perhaps a New Life

Summary

It is 1:00am on May 21, 2000, and Enrique is waiting by the edge of the water. El Tiríndaro will soon take him and two Mexican migrants, a brother and sister, across the Rio Grande. On the other side of the river stands a fifty-foot pole equipped with U.S. Border Patrol cameras. Patrol vehicles are nearby, but Enrique cannot see them in the dark. He and his companions strip to their underwear, and El Tiríndaro loads the Mexicans into a black inner tube and pushes them across the water to a small island halfway across the river. He then returns for Enrique.

They all know the dangers presented by the river - two nights before, a young migrant was killed when he was sucked into a whirlpool. In fact, fifty-four people had died that year in the Rio Grande near Nuevo Laredo. Enrique cannot swim, and is afraid. He holds onto the plastic bag filled with dry clothes and shoes as El Tiríndaro guides him across the river in the inner tube. Shortly after they arrive on the island, an SUV appears on the far bank, flashing red and blue lights and casting a spotlight on the island. Enrique and the others plaster themselves to the ground, and wait a half hour for the SUV to leave.

Immigrant children who are caught by the Border Patrol are sent to a Houston facility in shackles. There, they wait days in unsanitary conditions, with little food. The guards rarely speak Spanish, and the children have no idea when they will be deported. Some grow depressed and suicidal, while others stop eating altogether.

After the agents leave, El Tiríndaro takes them to shore. For the first time in his life and clothed only in his underwear, Enrique stands on U.S. soil. El Tiríndaro hides the inner tube and leads the group into a freezing cold creek filled with sewage. After waiting there for a half hour, they dress in their dry clothes from the plastic bags. El Tiríndaro gives them bread and soda. Once they are ready, El Tiríndaro leads them over a steep embankment and through other obstacles until they finally reach a two lane street. There, a Chevrolet Blazer flashes its lights.

The group jumps into the car, where a man and woman greet them. They are a part of El Tiríndaro's smuggling network. There are pillows in the back, onto which Enrique gladly falls asleep. He's awoken when their group has to leave the car so that the Blazer can pass through a U.S. checkpoint. They walk out of the way of the checkpoint, and regroup with the Blazer down the road. Enrique falls back to sleep. When he awakes again, El Tiríndaro is gone. Dawn arrives, and Enrique sees how beautiful and clean America is. After leaving the Mexicans somewhere, the driver brings Enrique to a house, where he changes into American clothing.

Meanwhile, Lourdes is waiting to hear from Enrique. She has not slept and worries for her son's life. A female smuggler calls and demands another $500. Lourdes wires the money to Western Union. Five days later, Enrique is driven to Orlando, Florida in a green van. Lourdes's boyfriend picks up Enrique there, and they drive to North Carolina. On May 28th, after traveling 122 days and over 12,000 miles, Enrique finally reunites with his mother. He bounds up the steps to Lourdes's trailer and runs inside to find his mother in bed. They hug and kiss, but they do not cry.

Nazario provides some perspective on the boy's journey. Unlike the heroes of the *Odyssey* and the *Grapes of Wrath*, whose stories end in reunion and peace, Enrique finds life with Lourdes to be difficult. Children like Enrique dream of finding their mothers and living happily ever after, but reality soon sets in. The children show resentment for being abandoned, especially when they confront the new families their mothers have made. They sometimes turn to drugs, pregnancies, early marriages, or gangs for comfort and approval. On the other hand, their mothers want respect for the sacrifices they have made over the years, and see their resentful children as ungrateful.

Enrique and Lourdes are no different, although their bond is strong. They live together in a trailer shared with several other people. At first, they eat and watch television together. Enrique gets to know Diana, his nine year old half-sister, and buys her gifts with money he earns as a painter and sander. Soon enough, though, he and Lourdes begin to clash. She wants him to study English; he wants to do as he pleases. One day, Lourdes's roommates reject a collect call from Marìa Isabel. Enrique is enraged, and packs to leave. Lourdes spanks him. Enrique locks himself in the bathroom, and later spends the night in a cemetery. They soon reconcile, but the difficulties persist. They have been away from one another for too long.

One day, Enrique learns that Marìa Isabel has given birth to a baby girl, whom they name Katerin Jasmín. Enrique encourages Marìa Isabel to come north, and she agrees to leave the baby behind.

Analysis

When Enrique stands for the first time in the United States, he is in his underwear, an image which reflects the crossroads between his past and future. His underwear is his final possession from home, and yet the baptism of the Rio Grande has presented him with a new life. It is telling that Enrique leaves the underwear behind when he moves on.

Like his two left shoes, Enrique is out of sync as he and the others navigate themselves through unfamiliar terrain until they reach their destination, a Chevrolet Blazer. Ultimately, though, they are lucky to have pillows and a mostly comfortable ride. Many smugglers stuff their charges into unimaginably tight spaces in cars and vans. Immigrants (usually small children) have been found in glove compartments, inside car seats where the interior has been removed, and even stuffed into car doors.

The pillows feel like heaven to Enrique after his long journey has comes to an end.

Nazario goes into great detail in relating the personality clashes that Lourdes and Enrique face. She expects respect and deference, but the very independence that helped him survive the journey is at odds with such expectations. The resentments that Nazario described when Enrique was still in Honduras now pay off in extreme ways, to the point that he is sometimes intentionally mean to his mother. She later reveals that ultimately, what he wants is an apology that she is unwilling to give. She, too, has suffered too much.

Despite his strong personality, Enrique's resentments reveal he is still a boy. He resents Diana, whom she sees as a representation of their riff, and cruelly tells his mother that her biggest mistake was getting pregnant with Diana. He argues that it was unwise to have another child when she struggled to provide for those she already had.

Their rift will grow more specific in the next chapter. Turning toward his favorite form of escapism, Enrique begins to drink, to sniff paint thinner, and misuse the steady money he now makes as a painter. In a role reversal, Enrique begins to neglect Marìa Isabel, and eventually Jasmìn. The similarities between his situation and Lourdes's are striking. When Lourdes arrived, she was able to send money home, but her diminished circumstances soon made that difficult. However, her pride kept her from being totally honest with her relations. Similarly, when he worked regularly, Enrique sent money to his family, but once he started drinking heavily, he too felt ashamed and stopped sending money home.

Marìa Isabel, in turn, finds herself in the position Lourdes once faced - that of a single mother who cannot afford to raise her child. She will soon face the same dilemma Lourdes did - do I risk losing the love of my child in order to provide for her? The patterns from the beginning of the book begin to repeat, suggesting that even Enrique's heroic success does not ensure a happy ending. Our protagonist has won the fight, and yet the fight now seems bigger and harder than ever.

Summary and Analysis of The Girl Left Behind and The Epilogue

Summary

The Girl Left Behind

Tensions between Enrique and Lourdes begin to rise. Enrique resents his mother for having left him, and says that "money does not solve anything" (197). He accuses her of loving Belky more than she did him, arguing Belky got a good home while he was left with an irresponsible father. He tells Lourdes that he considers his grandmother, Maria, to be his real mother. Lourdes tells Enrique that he should blame his father for leaving, and his grandmother for making him sell spices on the streets when he was a child. Lastly, she says he should blame himself for spending the money she sent him on drugs.

Mother and son become estranged. Enrique drinks more, and spends most of his money at topless bars. He does not send enough money to Jasmín. María Isabel waits for his phone call each Sunday, and is sometimes too emotional to speak over the phone. Enrique's family in Honduras, including his grandmother, sister, and three aunts, constantly criticize María Isabel's mothering. They say the baby is dirty, badly dressed, and too thin. They accuse María Isabel of misspending the money Enrique sends by buying her mother heart and asthma medicine, and by buying herself hair dye. María Isabel, having lived most of her life in complete poverty, feels justified in spending a bit of money on herself and her mother. She begins to deeply resent the interference of Enrique's family.

In the meantime, Enrique drinks more, and begins smoking marijuana again. He is caught speeding, and spends over a thousand dollars in court fines. He is not saving his money, although he wants to bring María Isabel north. Feeling desperate and depressed, Enrique begins to huff paint thinner. When Lourdes catches him in the act, she threatens to kick him out of the house. Enrique stops huffing paint thinner because it brings him extreme headaches - probably by exacerbating his injuries from the train beating - and not because his mother insists on it.

Back in Honduras, to escape the scrutiny of Enrique's family, María Isabel moves from her aunt Gloria's home to the home where her mother, Eva, lives. Eva's house is a hut on the side of a mountain in the small town of Los Tubos, but it has some conveniences that Gloria's did not. María Isabel gets a new job at a children's clothing store at the Mall Multiplaza, through which she earns $120 a month. Jasmín begins to put on more weight, and she speaks to her father over the phone for the first time on her second birthday.

Enrique has been in the United States for over two and half years. He resolves to do better, and wants to stop drinking. He does not want his daughter to grow up the way he did, always worried about money. He begins to work seven days a week, hoping to quickly earn enough money for a smuggler to bring María Isabel to the Untied States. His ultimate plan is they could raise money faster together in order to bring their daughter to them.

Lourdes' sister, Mirian, soon comes to the United States to live with them. She leaves her own three children behind in Honduras, but insists she will return as soon as she saves some money. Upset by the cramped conditions of his mother's apartment, Enrique moves out. Now, most of his money is budgeted for rent, car insurance, cell phone bills, and food.

Enrique sends less money to Honduras, but does not level with María Isabel about his difficulties. Her family encourages her to move on, to find someone else. Others tell her to go to the United States, while she is still young. In Honduras, middle-aged women have a hard time finding work that pays well, often settling for jobs that pay $50 to $90 a month. In 1998, Hurricane Mitch caused great devastation in Honduras, and caused an increase in unemployment that has only worsened. María Isabel understands both the benefits and dangers of leaving her native country, but most of all fears losing the love of her child.

Lourdes and her family, including Enrique, move to Florida to find better jobs. Enrique works as a painter, Lourdes as a maid. The arrangement does not work out for Enrique, and he soon returns to North Carolina to work with his friends. Lourdes is now able to afford an apartment alone with her boyfriend and Diana. While away from his mother, Enrique learns to empathize with her difficulties. He misses her, and returns to Florida to be with her. Although he does not entirely forgive Lourdes, Enrique has decided to stop living in the past, and to move on with his life.

Now, he saves in earnest for María Isabel to join him in the United States. In the spring of 2004, after four years in the United States, Enrique calls María Isabel and asks her to come north. He has saved enough money for a smuggler. Although María Isabel hesitates with her decision, she eventually leaves Honduras. She and Enrique will work together to create a better life for their daughter. The day María Isabel leaves with her smuggler, Jasmín cries *"Adiós mami"*, but has no idea that her mother will not be coming home (240).

The Epilogue

María Isabel travels through Mexico by bus with the help of her smugglers, who bribe Mexican law enforcement officers to let them pass. She safely arrives in Florida after a few weeks of travel. Jasmín has been left with Enrique's sister, Belky, who tells her plainly that her parents are not coming back, but hope to bring her to the United States one day. Enrique and María Isabel call their daughter once or twice a week, but Jasmín thinks of Belky's common-law husband as her father. Belky gives birth to a baby boy on July 31, 2006. She names him Alexander Jafeth.

The popular TV show *Don Francisco Presenta* features Enrique, Lourdes, and Sonia Nazario in one episode. Don Francisco surprises Lourdes by reuniting her with Belky, who has come to the United States on a temporary visa. It is the first time in eighteen years that Lourdes, Enrique, and Belky are together. It is also the first time that all three of Lourdes' children are in the same room, as Diana is in the audience. Belky leaves the United States eight days later to return to Honduras and her son.

Analysis

The theme of family drives this chapter, particularly in terms of the many miscommunications that occur between mother and son. Lourdes and Enrique cannot reach common ground, because neither can truly understand the other one's perspective. Lourdes will not apologize for her decision, because it was hard for her and was made for her children. Enrique will not appreciate her decision, because he feels betrayed. Enrique has successfully created a new life for himself in the United States but is it the life he has always wanted?

Enrique's new journey is one of self reflection. His drug use, harsh attitude, and resentments have created a divide in their relationship. Cramped living situations do not make it easier for him to gain any perspective. It is not until he is again separated from her, when he returns to North Carolina, that he can see outside himself. He remembers the years of separation, and feels the lonely side of independence. In coming to this realization, he not only chooses to return to Lourdes, but also commits fully to earning money for his own family. Ironically, by coming to this realization, he risks hurting Jasmìn the way he was hurt. Because he has grown more mature, he brings Marìa Isabel to the United States so they can help their daughter, but the circle will potentially repeat itself for her.

Sonia Nazario has kept in touch with Enrique, and updates the website dedicated to *Enrique's Journey* with information on his family. Since the publication of the book, Enrique, Marìa Isabel, and Jasmìn have been reunited in the United States. Jasmìn was smuggled north for the price of $5,000. She is very close to her grandmother, and follows Lourdes to work. Fluent in English, Jasmìn enjoys school and her favorite subject is math. She loves Justin Bieber and watches SpongeBob Squarepants and iCarly with her father.

Lourdes married her longtime boyfriend in May 2010. She became an Evangelical Christian, and hopes to become certified as a nursing assistant. She wants to own her own home, and dreams of Diana going to college.

Marìa Isabel works as a hotel maid making $7.50 an hour. At one point, she and Jasmìn moved in with Lourdes during a difficult period of her relationship with Enrique.

Enrique has had trouble maintaining a job, and continues to struggle with drug use. Both issues have been a source of contention with Marìa Isabel and his mother. Lourdes allowed Enrique to move in with her on the condition that he not use drugs in her home. Lourdes has faith that her son will one day change for the better.

For more information about Enrique and his family visit the author's website at www.enriquesjourney.com

Summary and Analysis of The Afterword: Women, Children, and the Immigration Debate

Summary

Approximately 1.7 million children live in the United States illegally, and have been separated from one or both parents at some point in their lives. One in four children in the U.S. public school system are immigrants or children of immigrants.

Today, children leaving Central America for the U.S. face a tougher journey than ever before. Chiapas is overrun with gangs ever since El Salvador, Honduras, and Guatemala pushed many of their gangsters north into Mexico. As a result, rampant violence in Chiapas has inspired the community to rise up and demand the death penalty for gangsters, although this has not helped the migrants. To deter the gangsters and the migrants, more police officers have been stationed in Chiapas; as a result, migrants take even greater risks in getting on and off the trains. The number of migrants being brought to the hospitals in Tapachula has doubled. In 2003, the La Arrocera checkpoint became too dangerous even for *la migra.* The train stop was moved to Los Toros in Chiapas, where police have reinforced their efforts to catch migrants, even using ladders to get to the tops of the trains.

In Nuevo Laredo, near the Rio Grande, a battle rages among the Mexican drug cartel who want control of the border. El Tiríndaro was found dead by the river, having been tortured and executed. Violence in the area has significantly escalated. In 2005, a newly elected police chief was gunned down because he advocated bringing law and order back to the city.

Sympathetic Mexicans have reported seeing more pregnant women and parents with young children aboard the freight trains than they had seen previously. Some of the children are babies. The number of Central American migrants detained and deported from Mexico each year has doubled since 2004. Divorce and separation is on the rise throughout all of Latin America, which promises to produce more single mothers, who in desperation will seek employment in the United States. The growing number of women and children entering the U.S. poses several questions: Is an increase in immigration good for the migrants? Is it good for the countries they left behind? Is it good for the United States? Nazario addresses each of these questions.

For migrants, the benefits far outweigh the risk. They are able to send much needed funds back to their families, thereby offering them a better life. Enrique says that although he feels the sting of racism in the U.S., he also enjoys its comforts. He has his own truck, and makes a decent living. Lourdes loves indoor plumbing and the safety her neighborhood provides. Both Enrique and Lourdes do acknowledge the drawbacks. They can be deported at anytime, and are paid lower wages then native born citizens.

Perhaps the largest downside of immigation is its impact on the nation's school system. Children who are reunited with their parent(s) in the United States become resentful, depressed, and rebellious in the classroom. Nearly half of all Central American children who arrive in the United States after the age of ten do not graduate from high school.

The countries that immigrants leave behind sometimes benefit. Immigrants send large sums of money back to their families, who in turn put that money back into the local economy, bringing about $30 billion a year to Latin America. Immigrants who return home bring new skills, education, and less tolerance for corruption. The telephone and internet systems in Central America have also improved because families want to communicate with their relatives in the U.S. A major negative impact, however, is the growing number of parentless children who end up in gangs. Government ads encourage parents to stay at home with children, and seek local jobs instead of emigrating to the United States.

Each year, approximately a million people enter the U.S. legally, while up to 700,000 enter illegally. Overall, immigration is higher than at any time in recent history. Experts say that the U.S. economy relies on the immigrants to provide a cheap labor which lowers the overall cost of American living. An opposing opinion suggests that immigrants tend to use more government assistance than native born citizens. They are poorer, and their generally large families require more to welfare, foot stamps, and Medicaid. Further, because they are either paid less or paid 'under the table,' their tax burden is lower than that of natives.

The influx of immigrants has impacted many public services, including schools, hospitals, and jails. Classrooms are overcrowded. Hospital emergency rooms have been forced to close because they are unable to meet the demands of a growing population that is unable to pay for care. The Los Angeles County jails have even released prisoners due to overcrowding. In 2001, the total cost of arresting, prosecuting, and jailing illegal immigrants amounted to $125 million. Immigrants amassed over $26.3 billion in government services in 2002, but paid only $16 billion in taxes.

In the 1980s, the RAND Corporation, a Santa Monica think tank, concluded that immigration influxes were beneficial. By 1997, they reserved their opinion. Some experts argue that it does not make sense to allow so many immigrants from underdeveloped nations to enter the United States, legally or otherwise. The U.S. needs to compete in a global market in industries that require high levels of education, and the average immigrant from Mexico has only completed a total of five to seven years of school. Poverty rates are doubling as the U.S. population continues to exponentially increase.

Two-thirds of Americas believe that the government should reduce the immigration levels and strengthen U.S. immigration policies which currently favor big businesses that employ legal and illegal immigrants at low wages. Attempts to strengthen the Border Patrol since 1993 have been mostly unsuccessful. More immigrants are using smugglers, or are entering the U.S. legally through the use of a temporary visa, and then staying illegally in the country. Experts suggest that the number of Central American immigrants entering the U.S. will decrease if and when the economies of Latin America rebound. Implementing more U.S. trade policies to aid Latin American economies could provide more jobs, and hence less incentive to emigrate. As one Honduran woman offers, "What would it take to keep people from leaving? There would have to be jobs. Jobs that pay okay. That's all" (260).

Analysis

The dangers of going north from Central America have significantly increased, and yet the number of migrants attempting the journey has doubled. The American Dream clearly lives on for these impoverished people. What has also changed is the type and age of people who risk the journey - as Nazario indicates, migrants are now seen traveling with children and even infants. This startling imagery speaks volumes. When Lourdes set out for the U.S., she paralleled her contemporaries who sought to provide a better life for their children by fulfilling the need for cheap domestic labor. Similarly, Enrique was one of many children who followed their mothers with no idea what to expect once they reached the United States.

Rumors, misinformation, even lies fuel the idea that jobs are plentiful in the U.S. Grupo Beta and other migrant rights groups try to educate migrants on not only the journey's dangers, but also on the divide between reality and expectation. Yet these efforts seem futile when paired next to the promise that migrants can realize the American Dream "over there." Hope remains the most powerful force.

Unfortunately, the streets of the United States are not paved with gold, and once the migrants cross the border and are rechristened as immigrants, they confront a whole new set of issues and hardships. Enrique and Lourdes are very open in admitting the presence of racism in the States. Mirian, Enrique's aunt, says she is paid less than her fellow employees who are native born citizens. Lourdes enjoys the comforts of the U.S., but recognizes the constant threat of deportation which looms over all illegal immigrants. She prays for papers that will grant her citizenship so that she might one day bring Belky to the United States.

Immigration is the primary theme of the book, and manifests on several different levels. It can be seen: on a personal level through Enrique's story; on a reflective level through Nazario's narration; and on a broader level through the collective impressions offered of migrants and citizens of both the U.S. and Central America. Especially in this Afterword, Nazario explores the various opinions that U.S. citizen hold on immigration. Nazario calls the U.S. immigration policies "schizophrenic" because they seem harsh but rarely deliver such harshness. She concludes that immigrants will continue to come so long as there are jobs here, and no jobs in their own countries.

There are many lessons to learn from *Enrique's Journey* about the broader issue of immigration, but the most important concerns the disintegration of family. As Nazario concludes, neither the children who are left behind nor those who follow their mothers ever fully recover from their ordeal. Their issues of abandonment, their anger, and their resentment influence their daily lives. Enrique turned to alcohol and drugs. Others turn to gangs and pregnancies. The mothers who left their children feel as if their sacrifices should be honored, and are confused when this does not happen. Nazario concludes *Enrique's Journey* with two parallel images. One is of young Jasmìn as she waves goodbye to her mother who is leaving for the United States. The other is of Belky as she returns to Honduras to raise her child. Although Nazario makes no personal judgments, and never breaks the narration of the text within the confines of the chapters, she uses the image of Belky boarding the plane to Honduras as a way to gently communicate to the reader that family must come first. As the advertisements from the government of Honduras state, it is time to stay home, to maintain the family.

Family, the most enduring theme throughout *Enrique's Journey*, perfectly concludes the story as Enrique is again reunited with his mother and now begins a new life with Marìa Isabel in the United States. Although they repeat Lourdes' "mistake" in leaving their child behind, we can only hope that the young couple will one day be reunited with their daughter either in the United States or back in Honduras. Our protagonist has reached his goal, but his struggles are not through.

Suggested Essay Questions

1. **Discuss the influx of single mothers from Central America and Mexico who illegally enter the United States. What is the cause of this phenomenon? How does it affect the United States?**

   Each year, the number of single mothers entering the U.S. illegally from Central America and Mexico grows. In turn, the number of children who follow them grows as well, and their cultural tendency towards large families often leads them to have children in the U.S. The increase in single female immigrants coincides with a rising divorce rate in Latin America; more mothers are left single and decide to travel north to compensate for a lost income and stability. Even though they work menial jobs (as maids, housekeepers, factory workers, nannies) for low pay, they require significant government assistance in the form of schools, hospitals, and prisons. These institutions are increasingly unable to meet the demands of such a large general population, which results in substandard care for all citizens who rely on those institutions. Also, the long periods of separation have a deep emotional impact on both mother and child. Children who find their mothers in the U.S. often cannot come to terms with their pasts, and find violent outlets for their resentments, which have lasting effects on the community at large.
2. **How does Lourdes's experience in the U.S. serve as a commentary on the American Dream?**

   When she was a child, Lourdes glimpsed images of the U.S. on television. She was enchanted by what she saw, and created for herself an image of prosperity that is often referred to as "the American Dream." However, Lourdes quickly realizes that the U.S. presents its own set of problems. She cannot rely on steady work, and even when she has it, racism and her illegal status limit her earning potential. Though she can send money home, her own pregnancy limits her ability to do so. Her economic potential is so low that she has to turn to a form of prostitution. Though Lourdes is able to prosper somewhat in the U.S., it requires significantly more sacrifice than "the American Dream" led her to expect, and also requires her to accept a certain sense of shame. The country is less open to immigrants than she had hoped.
3. **Why does Enrique turn to drugs for comfort?**

   Enrique's drug use can be understood in terms of his abandonment issues. Enrique is five years old when his mother leaves for the United States. He is shuffled from one family home to another, first that of his father, then that of his grandmother. He does not understand why his mother left, and then grows angry when her regular promises to return are not kept. As he grows older and develops an identity, it is an angry one - first, he acts out in school, and then later, he sniffs glue and is willfully disobedient to his elders. He is certainly a sensitive kid, which suggests that this behavior is more a form of escapism than hatred. He believes nobody loves him, and sees no solution to his resentment, so he turns to glue and marijuana for comfort. He continues to struggle with these addictions in the U.S., showing that geography cannot answer emotional pains.

4. **Why does Enrique decide to travel to the U.S.? Consider various reasons in your response.**

   The immediate impetus for Enrique's departure is his drug problem, but his decision can also be understood in terms of his strong penchant for hope and his personal strength. After his drug problem leaves him without a home, he makes plans to travel North and reunite with Lourdes. However, this plan had long been gestating in his mind. Enrique's issues - with drugs and anger - are easily connected to his abandonment issues, and as he shows through his persistence in attempting the journey eight times, he is not a quitter. When his circumstance in Honduras grow so bad that he cannot find anyone who loves him, he does not delve further into drugs but instead sets out on a dangerous journey, armed with few provisions outside of his hope and character. He idealizes Lourdes as his salvation, which could be understood as delusion but can also be seen as personal fortitude. He will not let the world beat him down.

5. **Describe the dangers that migrants face while traveling on the tops of freight trains.**

   The dangers of the trains are many, and include both physical and emotional struggles. Not only are the trains themselves dangerous, but migrants who travel on them must also overcome an onslaught of opposition. For instance, migrants can get pulled under the wheels while boarding the moving train, which can cause dismemberment or death. Others fall off the train while it is in motion. Gangs rule the train tops, robbing, beating, killing, and raping as they please. Migrants are also targeted by corrupt police and immigration authorities. Further, all decisions must be tempered by an ever-present threat of deportation. Both female and male migrants are in continual danger of rape. Migrants suffer from starvation and dehydration, and are unable to go to the bathroom for long periods of time. Children are often kidnapped by gangs or bandits for ransom money if they have a parent in the United States. Finally, all of this causes great emotional hurdles - there are so many reasons to turn back or seek deportation that only the strongest can persevere.

6. **Migrants use several different nicknames for the freight trains. Use examples to illustrate the meaning behind the monikers.**

   Migrants use several nicknames for the trains, each of which suggests a different outlook. Many call it *El Tren de la Muerte* (the Train of Death). This reflects a pessimism over the train's danger - many people die or are seriously wounded by it all the time, and must confront a multitude of other threats like bandits in order to survive. Another name that reflects this purpose is *El Tran Devorador* (The Train That Devours). Others call it the Pilgrim's Train, which indicates their extent of hope. They recognize a noble or spiritual purpose to the train that is bringing them to salvation in the North. Enrique prefers to call the train *El Caballo de Hierro* (the Iron Horse). What he recognizes is not its spiritual potential, but rather its physical strength.

7. **Discuss the treatment of Central Americans in Veracruz vs. their treatment in Mexico City.**

Whereas the migrants receive mercy and gifts in Veracruz, they are treated as undesirables in Mexico City. Men, women, and children run along the sides of the trains in Veracruz, throwing much needed clothing and food to the migrants aboard. The priests and bishops of Veracruz preach mercy and charity, saying that it is each citizen's Christian duty to help the Central American migrants. Many in this state stand up for the rights of migrants - they house them and allow them the use of their church. This kindness gives the migrants hope, and the faith to push forward on their journey, especially after the terrible treatment they suffer in Chiapas. Their treatment in Mexico City is remarkably different. The people of Mexico City are afraid of the migrants - they hear terrible stories about migrants stealing, propositioning young girls, raping boys, and more. They believe migrants bring disease, crime, and prostitution to the city and as a result, they shun Central American migrants. Though they are not outwardly vicious, they treat the migrants as undesirables.

8. **How is Enrique's family overly critical of María Isabel? How does this tie into the book's other themes?**

After Enrique leaves for the United States, María Isabel lives across the street from his sister, grandmother, and aunt. Enrique sends money to María Isabel to help pay for Jasmín's diapers, clothes, dry milk, and other necessities, but his support is watched closely by his relatives, who accuse María Isabel of negligence and greed. María Isabel admittedly does spend some of the money on herself and her mother, but having lived her entire life in poverty, she sees no shame in it. It is an unfortunate conflict between people whose lives are all hampered by poverty, but also indicates the way much-needed money can drive wedges between the poor. In even generosity is the potential for miscommunication.

9. **Discuss Enrique's resentment toward Lourdes after he arrives in North Carolina.**

Enrique makes an incredible journey to reunite with his mother, but quickly discovers that the truth of psychological damage is not easily addressed by idealized images. After Enrique arrives in the United States and settles into a new life with Lourdes, he quickly realizes his idealized version of his mother is inaccurate. She is practically a stranger to him, and he finds it difficult to manage his resentment and anger. He treats her cruelly, and sometimes explicitly accuses her of abandoning him and of not loving him. Despite the independence he showed on his journey, he regresses into a state of childish petulance in the way he lashes out at her, even for factors she cannot control, like the behavior of her roommates. The conflict poses another journey for Enrique, one in which he must come to peace with himself and his past. However, it also speaks to the lasting damage of abandonment, which in his case forces him to work through childhood feelings that had lain dormant for so long.

10. **According to leading immigration experts, how can the United States decrease the number of immigrants (legal and illegal) entering the country each year?**

    Immigration is a complicated issue, both in terms of its causes and effects. However, immigration experts, as quoted by Nazario, suggest that the best way to address it is by helping the third-world countries help themselves. If the United States forgave foreign debt to countries like Honduras, the borrowing nations could use that money to strengthen their economy and create new resources and new jobs. If new jobs were created, fewer people would feel compelled to leave their families in hope of prosperity elsewhere. Similarly, if the United States were to employ trade policies favoring these nations, more manufacturing opportunities might emerge. In short, the best way to address immigration is to eliminate the need for it, but the punitive policies of the U.S. cannot compete with individual desperation. The only way to succeed is to eliminate this desperation born from poverty.

The Shelter of Jesus the Good Shepherd

Sonia Nazario admirably tells her story without offering many moral judgments, and yet she does seems to be particularly impressed by The Shelter of Jesus the Good Shepard, which she visited for two weeks during her research. A noble institution devoted to migrants who have been severely injured by the train, the Shelter is worth understanding on its own terms, since it stands as a symbol of both the mercy and the danger that migrants face during their incredible journey north.

Located in Tapachula, Mexico, the shelter was founded by Olga Sánchez Martínez over twenty years ago. Most migrants who arrive at the shelter have lost limbs to the train. Nazario's Red Cross sources estimate that every two days, a migrant loses a limb to the train. This does not include the migrants who are killed while traveling.

Migrants fall from the train for several reasons - some fall asleep and tumble off the sides, while others are thrown by gangsters, or bandits. Some fall while trying to board, and are usually dragged under the wheels. Sometimes, the train makes a sharp turn that cause migrants to fall off. Low branches can also strike migrants.

Many of these injuries are treated by Mexican hospitals, but due to limited space and funding, patients are released before their treatment is complete. This is why institutions like The Shelter of Jesus the Good Shepherd are so important; they offer a temporary home for those tragically mauled by the trains. The shelter provides a place to stay and heal, and to find the strength to keep living. Because she faces so much skepticism over her noble purpose, Olga frequently tells her own story of how God saved her life and emboldened her to help others.

When Olga was diagnosed with cancer in 1990, she begged God to help her, promising she would devote her life to others if He did. Her cancer proved benign, and soon afterwards, she welcomed a young, legless Salvadoran boy into her home. She taught herself to wash and dress wounds, and eventually began to care for several other migrants whom the hospitals had rejected. Eventually, Olga, her husband, and volunteers were able to open the shelter. Over time, it has aided over 1,500 migrants.

To keep the migrants motivated, Olga and staff offer professional training sessions in English, computer skills, sewing, and other craft workshops. Most of the migrants were traveling to the U.S. to find work. Now they feel lost and ashamed, and do not want to return to their home countries despite injuries that will prohibit reaching the U.S. Olga and staff encourage patients to accept the conditions of their new life, and to find ways to go on. She sees her purpose as not just physical, but spiritual.

One of her main physical goals is locating prosthetic limbs. Since the shelter is run almost entirely through donations, it is difficult to pay for prosthetics, which can cost up to $2,000. Olga's tirelessness does yield dividends, however, and she has helped many limbless migrants.

To raise money for prosthetics, medicine, and institutional support, Olga and volunteers sell used clothing and baked goods. Although the shelter receives more migrants each year, its finances are not secure. The shelter relies heavily on donations. The cost of food, electricity, water, daily medical care, and upkeep is growing. As long as migrants ride the trains north, there will be injuries and a need for medical care.

To donate, visit The Shelter of Jesus the Good Shepherd's website at: http://www.alberguebuenpastor.org.mx/index.php/en/donations .

Author of ClassicNote and Sources

Melanie R. McBride, author of ClassicNote. Completed on August 19, 2012, copyright held by GradeSaver.

Updated and revised S.R. Cedars October 24, 2012. Copyright held by GradeSaver.

Roger Daniels. Guarding the Golden Door: American Immigration Policy and Immigrants Since 1882. New York: Hill and Wang A Division of Farrar, Straus, and Giroux, 2004.

Lynnaire M. Sheridan. "I Know It's Dangerous" Why Mexican Risk Their Lives to Cross the Border. Tucson: The University of Arizona Press, 2009.

Mariana van Zeller. "Amputee Shelter." Vanguard. 2006-01-04. 2012-08-13. <http://current.com/shows/vanguard/76279162_amputee-shelter.htm>.

William Etling, Laura Cavanaugh, Brandi Fowler, Melanie Roe, Shawna Thomas. "The Children Left Behind." News 21. 2006-08-04. 2012-08-09. <http://newsinitiative.org/story/2006/08/04/the_children_left_behind>.

"The Shelter." Albergue Jesus el Buen Pastor del Pobre y el Migrante. 2012-07-26. 2012-08-10. <http://www.alberguebuenpastor.org.mx/index.php/en/the-shelter>.

The Other Side of Immigration. Dir. Roy Germano. Roy Germano Films, 2010.

Which Way Home. Dir. Rebecca Cammisa. New Video Group, 2011.

Quiz 1

1. **Whose story inspired Sonia to write Enrique's Journey?**
   A. Gloria
   B. Maria
   C. Isabel
   D. Carmen

2. **Approximately how many immigrants enter the United States illegally each year?**
   A. 80,000
   B. 100,000
   C. 200,000
   D. 700,000

3. **Approximately how many immigrants enter the United States legally each year?**
   A. 1 million
   B. 10 million
   C. 800,000
   D. 750,000

4. **What type of employment is most common for female Latina immigrants?**
   A. Housecleaners
   B. Live in nannies
   C. Maids
   D. All of the above

5. **What country did Sonia's parents emigrate from?**
   A. Mexico
   B. Honduras
   C. Guatemala
   D. Argentina

6. **What did the Mexican authorities give Sonia to aid her investigation?**
   A. A personal attendant
   B. A letter from the personal assistant of the Mexican President
   C. A letter from the head of the Mexican Border Patrol
   D. A Mexican passport

7. **What color jacket does Sonia wear while investigating immigration?**
   A. Purple
   B. Red
   C. Blue
   D. Gray

8. **How many miles did Sonia travel in her quest to follow Enrique's journey?**
   A. 600
   B. 1,000
   C. 1,600
   D. 2,600

9. **How old is Enrique when Lourdes leaves for the United States?**
   A. 2
   B. 3
   C. 4
   D. 5

10. **Who does Enrique live with after Lourdes leaves for the United States?**
    A. His aunt
    B. His grandfather
    C. His father
    D. His neighbor

11. **After Enrique's father abandons him, who does he live with?**
    A. His stepmother
    B. His uncle
    C. His grandmother
    D. His cousin

12. **What is Lourdes's first official job after arriving in the United States?**
    A. Teacher
    B. Factory worker
    C. Housekeeper
    D. Live-in nanny

13. **Lourdes sends what kind of gifts to her children in Honduras?**
A. Clothes
B. Toys
C. Money
D. All of the above

14. **What does Enrique sell at an outdoor market when he is ten?**
A. Spices
B. Papayas
C. Tomatoes
D. Coconuts

15. **Who is Diana's father?**
A. Carlos
B. Victor
C. Santos
D. Marco

16. **After her boyfriend leaves with their life savings, Lourdes becomes a:**
A. Waitress
B. Maid
C. Prostitute
D. Nanny

17. **Enrique becomes addicted to what drug?**
A. Cocaine
B. Heroine
C. LSD
D. Marijuana

18. **In Honduras, what household product does Enrique sniff to get high?**
A. Paint thinner
B. Detergent
C. Glue
D. Permanent markers

19. **Why does Enrique steal jewelry from his Aunt?**
   A. To pay a smuggler
   B. To make his family angry
   C. To pay off his drug dealer
   D. To give to his girlfriend

20. **Who is Marìa Isabel?**
   A. Enriqueâ' s aunt
   B. Enriqueâ' s girlfriend
   C. Enriqueâ' s grandmother
   D. Enriqueâ' s sister

21. **How does Enrique celebrate his sixteenth birthday?**
   A. By jumping the trains
   B. By going to work
   C. By calling Lourdes
   D. By throwing a family party

22. **What causes Enrique to hallucinate?**
   A. Sniffing glue
   B. Falling off the train
   C. Illness
   D. A head injury

23. **Why can't Enrique hire a smuggler to take him north?**
   A. He does not trust smugglers.
   B. He cannot afford it.
   C. It is shameful to hire a smuggler.
   D. The smugglers do not like Enrique.

24. **Enrique writes his mother's phone number on a scrap of paper and on his _____.**
   A. Cap
   B. Underwear
   C. Jeans
   D. Shirt

25. **When does Enrique officially leave Honduras for the United States?**
   A. March 2, 2000
   B. March 2, 2002
   C. March 2, 2004
   D. March 2, 2007

Quiz 1 Answer Key

1. **(D)** Carmen
2. **(D)** 700,000
3. **(A)** 1 million
4. **(D)** All of the above
5. **(D)** Argentina
6. **(B)** A letter from the personal assistant of the Mexican President
7. **(B)** Red
8. **(C)** 1,600
9. **(D)** 5
10. **(C)** His father
11. **(C)** His grandmother
12. **(D)** Live-in nanny
13. **(D)** All of the above
14. **(A)** Spices
15. **(C)** Santos
16. **(C)** Prostitute
17. **(D)** Marijuana
18. **(C)** Glue
19. **(C)** To pay off his drug dealer
20. **(B)** Enrique's girlfriend
21. **(A)** By jumping the trains
22. **(A)** Sniffing glue
23. **(B)** He cannot afford it.
24. **(C)** Jeans
25. **(A)** March 2, 2000

Quiz 2

1. **Enrique is robbed of what items by the train gangsters?**
   A. His mother's phone number
   B. Money
   C. His clothing
   D. All of the above

2. **Why does the mayor decide to help Enrique?**
   A. Because it is his job to help the migrants
   B. Because he is a very charitable man
   C. Because it is cheaper to send him to the hospital than to bury him
   D. Because he knows Enrique and wants to help him

3. **How many migrants are deported from Mexico each year on the El Bus de Lágrimas?**
   A. 30,000
   B. 75,000
   C. 100,000
   D. 200,000

4. **Enrique was caught by la migra several times during his attempt to journey north. Which of the following incidences did not occur?**
   A. Enrique was caught by la migra while he slept on the train.
   B. Enrique was caught by la migra when he was sleeping on top of a mausoleum.
   C. Enrique was caught by la migra because he stopped at a diner to eat.
   D. Enrique was caught by la migra when he was eating alone near the Rio Grande.

5. **Which river does Enrique prefer to cross to get into Mexico?**
   A. RÃ−o Suchiate
   B. Rio Grande
   C. Rio Conchos
   D. Jamapa River

6. **In chapter 2, María Isabel wants to:**
   A. Journey north in search of Enrique
   B. Move in with Enriqueâ’ s family
   C. Pay off Enriqueâ’ s debts
   D. Get a job at a dress shop

7. **El Bus de Lágrimas deports migrants from Mexico to __________.**
   A. Honduras
   B. Costa Rica
   C. Guatemala
   D. El Salvador

8. **What injury does Enrique sustain at the hands of the six men on the train who beat him?**
   A. Head wound
   B. Lacerations
   C. Broken teeth
   D. All of the above

9. **Which southern state of Mexico do migrants call "the beast?"**
   A. Chiapas
   B. Yucatan
   C. Campeche
   D. Oaxaca

10. **Where does Enrique hide in Chapter 3 after he is arrested by la migra?**
   A. In a tree
   B. A cemetery
   C. Behind a parked car
   D. An abandoned house

11. **The average age of children taking the journey north through Tapachula is:**
   A. 12
   B. 14
   C. 15
   D. 16

12. **Which of the following is not a term associated with freight trains?**
   A. Hopper
   B. Cockpit
   C. Boxcars
   D. Round Compressor

13. **What does El Tren de la Muerte translate to?**
    A. The Train of Hope
    B. The Train of Iron
    C. The Train of Death
    D. The Train of Sorrow

14. **Why is the La Arrocera check point so dangerous?**
    A. La migra have been known to shoot fleeing migrants.
    B. It is isolated with few hiding places for migrants.
    C. Bandits patrol the area, ready to rob and murder.
    D. All of the above

15. **The gangs control the tops of the trains. Why is Enrique protected by the MS gang?**
    A. He is an informant for the gang.
    B. He joins the gang.
    C. He befriends a member of the gang.
    D. His cousin is a gang member.

16. **How do women NOT protect themselves on the trains?**
    A. They carry mace.
    B. They pretend to be boys.
    C. They strap their breasts down.
    D. They cut their hair.

17. **In Mexico, agua translates to:**
    A. T-shirt
    B. Soda
    C. Water
    D. Jacket

18. **How much do prosthetic limbs generally cost in Mexico?**
    A. $3,000
    B. $5,200
    C. $1,800
    D. $2,500

19. **Olga believes God cured her of what disease?**
   A. Scarlet Fever
   B. Addison's disease
   C. Cancer
   D. Multiple Sclerosis

20. **What symbol does Enrique see upon his arrival in Veracruz?**
   A. A painting of the Virgin Mary
   B. A church
   C. A statue of Jesus
   D. A monastery

21. **Many Christian migrants carry what text with them in plastic bags?**
   A. An English dictionary
   B. The Bible
   C. The Torah
   D. The Quran

22. **The _______ Psalm begins "Yea though I walk through the valley of the shadow of death…"**
   A. Forty-Eighth Psalm
   B. Ninety-First Psalm
   C. Twenty-Third Psalm
   D. Thirty-Second Psalm

23. **What type of food does Enrique receive from the kind people of Veracruz?**
   A. Rolls of bread
   B. Bananas
   C. Lemonade
   D. A bag of beans

24. **Which Gospel of the Bible preaches charity and compassion toward strangers?**
   A. Matthew
   B. Mark
   C. John
   D. Luke

25. **Priests in Veracruz tell parishioners to help migrants, saying that even ________ once fled from Israel into Egypt.**

A. St. Paul

B. St. Matthew

C. St. John the Baptist

D. Jesus Christ

Quiz 2 Answer Key

1. **(D)** All of the above
2. **(C)** Because it is cheaper to send him to the hospital than to bury him
3. **(C)** 100,000
4. **(C)** Enrique was caught by la migra because he stopped at a diner to eat.
5. **(A)** Río Suchiate
6. **(A)** Journey north in search of Enrique
7. **(C)** Guatemala
8. **(D)** All of the above
9. **(A)** Chiapas
10. **(B)** A cemetery
11. **(C)** 15
12. **(B)** Cockpit
13. **(C)** The Train of Death
14. **(D)** All of the above
15. **(C)** He befriends a member of the gang.
16. **(A)** They carry mace.
17. **(C)** Water
18. **(C)** $1,800
19. **(C)** Cancer
20. **(C)** A statue of Jesus
21. **(B)** The Bible
22. **(C)** Twenty-Third Psalm
23. **(A)** Rolls of bread
24. **(A)** Matthew
25. **(D)** Jesus Christ

Quiz 3

1. **Why were protesters angry at the hospitals in Veracruz?**
   A. The hospital refused to treat a migrant boy who lost a foot when he fell from a train.
   B. Hospital staff allowed la migra to deport injured migrants before they were healed.
   C. The hospital refused to treat any migrants.
   D. The hospital would not release migrants until they paid for treatment.

2. **What agreement was made between the church and the police/la migra in Veracruz?**
   A. The police/la migra were no longer allowed to deport migrants.
   B. The police/la migra will not beat or rob migrants.
   C. The police/la migra must now provide food and clothing for all migrants.
   D. The police/la migra cannot go into the church to hunt down migrants.

3. **What item is NOT stolen from Enrique by the police in Córdoba?**
   A. A cap
   B. A belt
   C. His mother's number
   D. Money

4. **How much money does Enrique make on his first day while working for the brick maker?**
   A. 30 pesos
   B. 40 pesos
   C. 50 pesos
   D. 80 pesos

5. **What is a combi?**
   A. A train
   B. A truck
   C. A minibus
   D. A car

6. **How does Enrique travel to Nuevo Laredo?**
   A. He walks.
   B. He steals a horse.
   C. He hitchhikes on a truck.
   D. He takes a bus.

7. **Why is Enrique overwhelmed when he sees the United States across the Rio Grande?**
    A. He realizes he does not know what his mother looks. like anymore
    B. He thinks the United States is a mystery.
    C. He is tired from traveling.
    D. All of the above

8. **How many days does it take Enrique to reach the Rio Grande on his eighth attempt north?**
    A. 25 days
    B. 53 days
    C. 47 days
    D. 104 days

9. **How does Enrique raise money to buy the phone cards?**
    A. He works in a factory.
    B. He washes cars.
    C. He sells tacos.
    D. He cleans apartments.

10. **How much did Enrique pay for two phone cards?**
    A. 20 pesos
    B. 30 pesos
    C. 50 pesos
    D. 100 pesos

11. **What is referred to as la cura (the cure)?**
    A. Cocaine
    B. Heroine
    C. LSD
    D. Marijuana

12. **What does Enrique do to starve off hunger, fear, and loneliness in Nuevo Laredo?**
    A. He walks by the river.
    B. He sniffs glue.
    C. He stares at the stars.
    D. He sleeps too much.

13. **What does Enrique's tattoo say?**
    A. EnriqueMariaIsabel
    B. EnriqueJasmin
    C. EnriqueEnrique
    D. EnriqueLourdes

14. **Why are the trains that travel from Mexico to Texas so dangerous for migrants?**
    A. Dogs search the trains.
    B. The trains are inspected several times.
    C. The trains are scanned by infrared telescopes.
    D. All of the above

15. **How many pairs of shoes does Enrique go through on his journey north?**
    A. 7
    B. 9
    C. 10
    D. 12

16. **What color is Padre Leo's bicycle?**
    A. Orange
    B. Red
    C. Blue
    D. Green

17. **Who gives Enrique his mother's phone number?**
    A. MarÃ–a Isabel
    B. His old boss at the tire store
    C. Padre Leo
    D. Uncle Carlos and Aunt Rosa Amalia

18. **What does Enrique wear on his feet after one of his shoes is stolen?**
    A. Two left shoes
    B. Two right shoes
    C. Paper bags
    D. Plastic bags

19. **Who smuggles Enrique across the border?**
    A. Lourdesâ' s boyfriend
    B. El TirÃ–ndaro
    C. El Brujo
    D. Padre Leo

20. **How does Enrique cross the Rio Grande?**
    A. By boat
    B. By canoe
    C. By taking an inner tube
    D. By swimming

21. **What is in the plastic bag that Enrique carries with him across the river?**
    A. Dry clothes and shoes
    B. A fake passport
    C. His mother's phone number
    D. Money

22. **Why is Enrique afraid of crossing the Rio Grande?**
    A. He cannot swim.
    B. The whirlpool may pull him under.
    C. He does not want to be caught and deported.
    D. All of the above

23. **What saint does Lourdes pray to for Enrique's safety?**
    A. St. Paul
    B. St. Joseph
    C. St. Jude
    D. St. Judas Tadeo

24. **In the end, how much does Lourdes pay for Enrique's safe return?**
    A. $1,200
    B. $1,500
    C. $1,700
    D. $1,800

25. **What books does Nazario compare Enrique's journey to?**

A. Moby Dick & Great Expectations
B. Middlemarch & The Invisible Man
C. The Odyssey & The Grapes of Wrath
D. Wuthering Heights & Pride and Prejudice

Quiz 3 Answer Key

1. (**B**) Hospital staff allowed la migra to deport injured migrants before they were healed.
2. (**D**) The police/la migra cannot go into the church to hunt down migrants.
3. (**C**) His mother's number
4. (**D**) 80 pesos
5. (**C**) A minibus
6. (**C**) He hitchhikes on a truck.
7. (**D**) All of the above
8. (**C**) 47 days
9. (**B**) He washes cars.
10. (**C**) 50 pesos
11. (**B**) Heroine
12. (**B**) He sniffs glue.
13. (**D**) EnriqueLourdes
14. (**D**) All of the above
15. (**A**) 7
16. (**C**) Blue
17. (**D**) Uncle Carlos and Aunt Rosa Amalia
18. (**A**) Two left shoes
19. (**B**) El Tiríndaro
20. (**C**) By taking an inner tube
21. (**A**) Dry clothes and shoes
22. (**D**) All of the above
23. (**D**) St. Judas Tadeo
24. (**C**) $1,700
25. (**C**) The Odyssey & The Grapes of Wrath

Quiz 4

1. **What news does María Isabel give Enrique at the end of Chapter 6?**
   A. She is moving out of her home.
   B. Sheâ' s pregnant.
   C. She got a job.
   D. She is on her way to North Carolina.

2. **Who tells Lourdes, "money doesn't solve anything?"**
   A. Mirian
   B. Enrique
   C. Diana
   D. Belky

3. **Who does Enrique call his "real mother?"**
   A. Mirian
   B. His grandmother Maria
   C. Rosa Amalia
   D. Belky

4. **Who is Katerin Jasmín?**
   A. Enriqueâ' s stepsister
   B. Enriqueâ' s niece
   C. Enriqueâ' s cousin
   D. Enriqueâ' s daughter

5. **Enrique sleeps on the ______ at Lourdes's American home.**
   A. Bed
   B. Sofa
   C. Chair
   D. Floor

6. **Lourdes claims she would often refuse to send Enrique money because he might:**
   A. Spend it at a bar
   B. Spend it on drugs
   C. Give it away
   D. Use it to come north

7. **What vice does Enrique turn to as an escape from Lourdes's anger?**
   A. Alcohol
   B. Robbery
   C. Gambling
   D. Joyrides

8. **Lourdes and her family move from North Carolina to _________to find work.**
   A. Florida
   B. South Carolina
   C. Tennessee
   D. Mississippi

9. **Why does Enrique stop sniffing paint thinner?**
   A. The doctor tells him to stop.
   B. He no longer can get high from it.
   C. He cannot afford paint thinner.
   D. He gets extreme headaches.

10. **Who does María Isabel move in with to escape the criticism of Enrique's family?**
    A. Her aunt
    B. Her uncle
    C. Her grandmother
    D. Her mother

11. **At what age does Jasmín speak to her father for the first time?**
    A. 2
    B. 3
    C. 4
    D. 5

12. **How much money does Enrique hope to save to build a house and start a business in Honduras?**
    A. $40,000
    B. $50,000
    C. $70,000
    D. $80,000

13. **María Isabel travels with her smugglers mostly on:**
    A. Trains
    B. Airplanes
    C. Cars
    D. Buses

14. **Jasmín thinks her father is:**
    A. Belkyâ’ s husband
    B. Her grandfather
    C. Uncle Marco
    D. Uncle Carlos

15. **Enrique, Lourdes, and Sonia Nazario were featured on what popular Spanish television show?**
    A. VersiÃ³n EspaÃ±ola
    B. Don Francisco Presenta
    C. El Gordo y la Flaca
    D. Buenafuente

16. **Who is the surprise guest on the Spanish television show?**
    A. MarÃ–a Isabel
    B. JasmÃ–n
    C. Eva
    D. Belky

17. **Lourdes was separated from Belky for how many years?**
    A. 12
    B. 15
    C. 16
    D. 18

18. **How many children live illegally in the U.S.?**
    A. 11 million
    B. 1.7 million
    C. 2.8 million
    D. 17 million

19. **In 2004, fed up with rampant gang violence, residents of Tapachula demanded ______ for gangsters.**
    A. life in prison
    B. the death penalty
    C. community service
    D. deportation

20. **Across Mexico, people who help the migrants have seen more ________ on the freight trains.**
    A. Animals
    B. Pregnant women
    C. United States citizens
    D. Dead babies

21. **The _______ rate in Latin America forces single mothers to seek employment in the U.S.**
    A. Divorce
    B. Marriage
    C. Death
    D. Birth

22. **The author calls U.S. immigration policies:**
    A. Bipolar
    B. Schizophrenic
    C. Outlandish
    D. Ridiculous

23. **Recent polls indicate that more Americans believe the government should:**
    A. Reduce immigration from current levels
    B. Increase immigration from current levels
    C. Allow states to dictate immigration policy
    D. Increase the number of agents in Border Patrol

24. **The amount of money immigrants send to family members in their home countries amounts to _______ a year.**
    A. 30 billion
    B. 30 million
    C. 30 thousand
    D. 30 trillion

25. **Nazario suggests that _______ in Central America would cause the immigration rate to lower.**

   A. Higher salaries

   B. Jobs

   C. A new leader

   D. A lower divorce rate

Quiz 4 Answer Key

1. (**B**) She's pregnant.
2. (**B**) Enrique
3. (**B**) His grandmother Maria
4. (**D**) Enrique's daughter
5. (**B**) Sofa
6. (**B**) Spend it on drugs
7. (**A**) Alcohol
8. (**A**) Florida
9. (**D**) He gets extreme headaches.
10. (**D**) Her mother
11. (**A**) 2
12. (**B**) $50,000
13. (**D**) Buses
14. (**A**) Belky's husband
15. (**B**) Don Francisco Presenta
16. (**D**) Belky
17. (**D**) 18
18. (**B**) 1.7 million
19. (**B**) the death penalty
20. (**B**) Pregnant women
21. (**A**) Divorce
22. (**B**) Schizophrenic
23. (**A**) Reduce immigration from current levels
24. (**A**) 30 billion
25. (**B**) Jobs

Made in the USA
Lexington, KY
17 July 2016